Getaway GUIDE TO
Fly-fishing
in South Africa

Nigel Dennis

SUNBIRD
PUBLISHING

IN ASSOCIATION WITH GETAWAY

First published 2004
2 4 6 8 10 9 7 5 3 1
Sunbird Publishing (Pty) Ltd
34 Sunset Avenue, Llandudno, Cape Town, South Africa
Registration number: 4850177827

Publisher Dick Wilkins
Editor Brenda Brickman
Designer Mandy McKay
Production Manager Andrew de Kock

Reproduction by Unifoto (Pty) Ltd, Cape Town
Printed and bound by Tien Wah Press (Pte) Ltd, Singapore

ISBN: 1 919 93812 5

PREVIOUS PAGE The delights of small-stream fishing: nymphing a productive run on the Little Mooi.
ABOVE A classic attractor dry fly, the Humpy will often trigger a rise even when no insects are hatching.
OPPOSITE A deep plunge pool at the base of a waterfall is an excellent spot to try for a big fish with a weighted nymph.

CONTENTS

ACKNOWLEDGEMENTS

Firstly, sincere thanks to my wife Wendy for taking many of the images in this book. Wendy is a little shorter than I am, so when I was wading thigh deep in fast-flowing streams, she was often up to her waist in icy water and carrying a bag full of very expensive photographic equipment. Fortunately, we managed to complete the assignment without any mishaps!

Thanks to Roger Baert, Michael Greene, Basil Hancock, Linda Hill and André Robins for acting as fly-fishing photographic 'models'; special thanks to Roger for being kind enough to write the foreword to this book, and for his useful advice while the work was in progress. Roger is widely credited as having introduced float tubing to this country. I have to say also that he is one of the true gentlemen of South African fly-fishing.

My gratitude to The Natal Fly Fishers Club for providing many years of enjoyable, affordable trout fishing.

Thanks also to the many landowners who kindly allowed us access to their property. Some of the images were taken on private waters, where the owners have asked not to be named – so, an anonymous 'thank you'.

The majority of the photographs were taken on waters that allow fishing access to those renting accommodation. My thanks to: Drayton Farm (tel: 033 266 6114), Dondini Trout Cottages (tel: 0332 677108), Lake Naverone (tel: 033 701 1236), Sani Valley Lodge (tel: 033 702 0203), Springholm (tel: 033 266 6074), Tillietudlem Trout Fishing (tel: 033 2344226)

Nigel Dennis

NIGEL DENNIS

TOP The journey in pursuit of trout takes us to some of South Africa's most scenically inspiring areas. Set against the spectacular Drakensberg escarpment, Erskine Dam in the upper Kamberg valley has long been a favourite venue for visiting anglers.

FOREWORD

I have often fished with Nigel and, as fishing buddies, we do tend to take the mickey out of each other at every possible opportunity ... myself by carefully annotating fishing returns, with consummate details of my prowess in outfishing him (which, so far, has happened all of once), and he by describing somewhere in this book how I prefer to land trout with a bra, instead of a landing net ...

I must admit, however, that Nigel does catch fish. Many fish. And big ones too. But, unbelievably, this outstanding wildlife photographer, whose books you can find in every bookshop in South Africa, only started taking a camera onto the water very recently – after he decided to write this book. And then again, most of the time, Wendy, his understanding better half, has had to hold the camera for him because shutter manipulations, light intensity and all that sort of thing are far less important in Nigel's fly-fishing mind than outwitting trout. And when Nigel fly-fishes he fly-fishes – period.

Nigel has managed to concentrate into this relatively small book that part of his vast knowledge and experience of fly-fishing which is of most use to South African anglers,

beginners and advanced alike. I, for one, have picked up from these pages a number of things that had never occurred to me and could only have been known to a truly passionate and constantly observant fly-fisher. Did you know, for instance, that in dams, fish tend to cruise the surface upwind (and make the return trip back down the dam, swimming deeper); so, in a ripple, it is usually a good bet to place your dry fly well upwind of the last rise? Likewise, many advanced South African fly-fishers will do well to heed Nigel's advice on leaders, tippets and the use of two-fly rigs.

Finally, there is a lot in this book that will please the fly-tier: the flies that Nigel has settled on recommending to us (from the incredibly vast array he has tried and tested) are all flies that truly work, and should be infallible if correctly *tied*, *presented* and *retrieved*. I believe that Nigel's most forceful tip to SA fly-fishers, although never stated in as many words, is simply, 'it ain't the fly you use, it's the way you use it.'

Roger Baert
The Flyfisherman, Hilton

These are just three of my many fly boxes, crammed with over 100 patterns tied in a range of sizes. But do you really need so many flies? Probably not, as I catch the great majority of my trout on a core collection of less than 20 carefully chosen patterns.

A very prestigious London fly-fishing club has, as their motto, the often-quoted phrase, 'there is more to fishing than catching fish' – only in Latin, of course. This is, indeed, an apt observation, particularly here in South Africa, where the journey in pursuit of trout takes us through and to some of the most scenically inspiring areas that the country has to offer – pristine mountain streams and high-altitude, crystal-clear dams in settings that would do justice to any calendar.

So does it really matter if we catch trout at all?

A short while ago, I called in at the local fly-fishing store in Hilton – The Flyfisherman, where I am very much a regular. As usual, co-owner Roger Baert was in residence, along with Maxi Holder, a very accomplished fly-fisher with a knowledge of trout fodder (aquatic insects) that is simply astounding. During a quiet moment at the shop we knocked this topic around a bit.

The verdict was unanimous – yes, it *is* wonderful just to be out on trout water, but we were adamant that fishing is a lot more fun when we *do* actually catch fish.

Hence the production of this book. A simple, no-nonsense nuts-and-bolts guide to help you catch more trout. All the aesthetic stuff about the wonder of nature is also very important of course. It will hit you when you take a moment to look around you – you certainly don't need a book to tell you that.

I would like to stress that few of the ideas in this book are my own. I admit that I am an avid collector of fly-fishing literature, and I have a bookcase full of books on the subject, as well as kilos of fly-fishing magazines. My point being, that if you are not careful, this off-shoot of the hobby can become more expensive than actually going fishing!

While we have many very skilled trout fisherfolk in this country, the main innovative advances in modern fly-fishing techniques have come from America and Europe, which is why I like to keep abreast of what is going on over there. And in this book I have attempted to compile the best of the ideas that have evolved abroad over the past couple of decades – or at least those that are appropriate to local fishing conditions and have worked well for me. I hope at the very least that this book will provide you with a few fresh ideas.

While we're on the subject, trout fishing in South Africa is often compared unfavourably to that in New Zealand, Patagonia, Alaska ... wherever. Perhaps our trout fishing isn't quite at the top of the world league, but I don't think we are too far off. Our best still waters produce trout of a size that would be considered true trophies just about anywhere. And, although South African rivers do suffer during drought cycles, in good wet times I think they measure up pretty well. Certainly we don't get the huge river trout that attract legions of anglers to New Zealand, but we make up for that in quantity because of large numbers of average-sized fish that can be found in our streams.

The nicest thing about local trout fishing is that it is affordable – unlike much of Europe, where the costs involved are simply exorbitant. I remember my frustration when I lived in Britain, where first-class chalkstream fishing was unquestionably beyond my means – even though I earned a fair salary at the time.

We also have a *lot* of accessible water. An angler who parked himself in Rhodes, for example, might fish every day for the entire season, and still not manage to properly cover all the region's available Wild Trout Association streams.

Where our trout fishing does differ from that in many other parts of the world is that we rarely experience enormous single-species fly hatches. Being in Africa, we do, of course, have lots of bugs, but many species tend to be present simultaneously. On my local dams (in KwaZulu-Natal), I have seen hatches of caddis, mayfly and midge, along with terrestrials – beetles, ants and grasshoppers – *all* on the water at the same time. For this reason our trout tend to be less fly-pattern selective than you might expect elsewhere. I have featured just 21 carefully chosen fly patterns in this book – and I think that is about all that you will really need to catch plenty of trout in our local waters. Rationalising a fly selection is a good way to cut through the complexity of modern fly-fishing.

Having said that, rather than being fly-pattern orientated, this book focuses on finding trout, and making the appropriate presentation. I believe that this is the essence of successful trout fishing in South Africa.

South African trout fishing can be very affordable. Here I have just netted a respectable-sized rainbow from a club dam, where annual membership costs less than a good-quality fly line.

Many of our dams are stocked with fry or fingerling trout, creating a feeling of 'wildness'. The result is pristine, hard-fighting 'grown-on' fish in prime condition.

Medium-action rods offer the best of both worlds: a crisp casting action, as well as the ability to play fish hard without breaking the tippet or having the hook pull out. Here I am able to really lean into a lively 5-pounder, hooked on a light tippet and a size 14 nymph.

RODS

My early fishing experiences date back to the days of fibreglass and split cane. Fibreglass was cheap but heavy, and a bit tiring to cast, especially in the long-distance department. Split cane – at least the good stuff – was dreadfully expensive, and also rather on the heavy side. The result, after a long day's fishing, was usually a sore arm and wrist! Then along came graphite, featherweight in comparison, and with an amazingly quick recovery from loading. Suddenly it was easy to generate high line speed and most anglers found they were able to cast further with less effort. Graphite rods are now in their fourth decade of development, and just keep getting better and better.

Rod action

Essentially, there are three classes of rod action: slow, medium (also called progressive action, or mid-flex, by some rod manufacturers – just to confuse us all!), and fast. Choosing the right rod is critical if you want to get maximum enjoyment from your fishing.

A 2-weight rod is ideal when a delicate presentation with small flies is called for. A medium-action 2 weight has sufficient power to play fish quickly and cope with light winds when casting.

Slow rods are excellent for playing fish, as they bend right down to the butt and have plenty of dampening action to protect light tippets. Unfortunately, they tend to have a rather sloppy action and are not easy to master, even at medium range. Also, they are best suited to short-range deep nymphing in big rivers – a technique seldom needed here, so I think we can rule them out of the equation for most South African trout fishing.

Very **fast, tip-action rods** came into fashion in a big way a few years back. The idea is that their quick recovery from loading generates high line speed so you can, in theory, cast much further. However, to get the most out of a very fast rod, your timing and style have to be impeccable. I too went through the fast rod fad, but found that although I made longer casts, it required a lot of concentration. I also found that very fast rods require more care in playing fish and striking, because the 'give' in the rod is restricted to the top few feet. I was certainly breaking off on more fish.

Although some well-known and respected local anglers still favour fast rods, these days I use only **mid-action rods** for all my fishing. These do, however, have a tendency to be just a tad on the fast side to maintain a crisp casting stroke, so they cast easily with little effort. 'Forgiving' would be an apt description; even if casting timing is a little out, a medium-action rod will still throw a fair line. The progressive taper also has a good dampening effect when fighting fish. In fact, I believe I can play a fish much harder using a mid-action rod (without breaking the tippet or having the hook pull out) than I could with the very fast rods. So, for my money, medium-action rods are the best compromise and certainly the way to go for local conditions.

Line weight and rod length

The next question concerning rod choice is line weight and rod length. If you fish mainly in dams, a 5 weight would be a good option. Personally, I don't own anything heavier, but if you do lots of bank fishing on large still waters, you might consider going up to a 6 – just to get a little more punch on a windy day. Much of my dam fishing is from float tubes and kick boats, and these allow me to fish downwind – or at least crosswind – most of the time, so the 5 weight works fine. Also, a 5 weight is about the lightest rod that will cast large, heavy, wind-resistant flies such as size 8 Woolly Buggers and Zonkers.

I also carry a 4 weight for floating line nymphing and dry-fly fishing on still waters. I use this extensively when a more delicate presentation with small flies is required. The 4 weight is also the perfect river rod for all but the very

Traditionally, small streams are fished with 7$\frac{1}{2}$-foot rods. These days, I frequently opt for a 9 foot 4 weight – which allows me to pitch a heavy nymph and get deep down in the swirling currents.

smallest streams. Both my 5 and 4 weights are 9-footers. The 'standard' rod length in these line weights is 8$\frac{1}{2}$ feet. That little extra length makes casting much easier from the low position of a float tube or kick boat. When on a river, the 4-weight 9-foot rod allows me to throw a high back cast to avoid hooking up on tall grass and bushes behind me (well, sometimes!). Also, roll casts and line mends are easier with the long rod – and these are techniques constantly used in river fishing.

And what of the **ultra-light rods**? Over the years, we have seen the lightest rods on the market come down from 2 weight, to 1 weight, and very recently, to 0 weight. The 1 and 0 weights are very specialised tools designed for catching small trout in small streams. Even so, you need a perfect, calm day to cast such light gear. Some folk love these featherweights, but I consider their use so limited that I have never felt the urge to make the investment.

Modern 2-weight rods are, to my mind, about as light as you can go and still have a versatile, practical fishing tool. My 2 weight is 8 foot 4 inches, mid- to slightly fast action, weighing just 2$^7/_8$ ounces.

I bought it mainly for small stream fishing – even a 1-pounder can show off rather nicely on such light gear. I also use it often on still waters for stalking with small nymphs and delicate dry-fly work. This rod has a surprising amount of power in the butt section – certainly enough to control a decent-sized fish. I have taken a couple of 9-pound rainbows on my 2 weight, and was able to land them quickly enough to release them successfully.

I have heard that you should not attempt to release big fish on light rods. I disagree, and am convinced that tippet strength and hook sizes are the determining factors in landing a fish quickly. If you fish a 6× tippet with a size 20 fly, then you are going to have to play a fish very gently, no matter what rod you use. I often fish a 3× fluorocarbon tippet with a size 12 strong, heavy wire hook on my 2 weight, and can put some *serious* pressure on a big trout. I have to admit that the rod does take on an alarming bend, such that the 25-year unconditional warranty on my Orvis is very reassuring!

Local or imported?

Should you buy local or imported rods? Locally produced rods, such as Stealth and Deane, are enormously popular and, with very affordable entry-level prices, they offer outstanding value. The main problem that I have with local rods is that the popular trout weights – the 4s and 5s – are mostly only available as 8½-foot models. So you lose out on that '9-foot advantage' I mentioned earlier. I understand that there are plans to introduce locally produced 9- and even 10-foot 5-weight rods in the future, so the situation may have changed by the time you read this.

An imported rod from one of the 'big names', such as Sage, Loomis, Orvis, Thomas & Thomas, Hardy, and so on, will cost you between five and 12 times as much as the local

High water on the Upper Lotheni River. I made a tactical error by taking only my ultra-light 2-weight rod, making it almost impossible to cast the heavy nymph rigs necessary under such conditions. A heavier outfit would have been better suited to coping with the strong flow.

A selection of midge pupa and larva patterns. Foam fly boxes are ideal for storing nymphs and streamers. Their only disadvantage is that barbless hooks tend to come loose, so it is a good idea to de-barb hooks only when you start to fish.

product. One thing I can guarantee you is that you will not catch five to 12 times as many fish with these rods! You will, however, be buying into decades of very extensive research and fine-tuned rod-building experience. Overall, imported rods tend to be lighter, and give at least some advantage in casting performance. Something to watch out for is that some top-of-the-range imported rods may be built on exactly the same blank as the mid-priced models. In other words, you might be paying an awful lot of extra cash just to get slightly better quality rod guides and a cork handle – albeit flashier in appearance!

This is where a good tackle dealer will be able to advise you on which model to choose to get the best value for money.

Try before you buy

The last word on rods is, never buy until you have tried casting with the entire setup – this means using the reel and line you intend to fish with the outfit. Many of the better fly-fishing shops have demo rods or even casting pools, so you can try before you buy. Spending a fortune on a snazzy imported rod does not necessarily mean it will be suited to your personal casting style, so be sure it is the right rod for you before parting with all that cash.

REELS

I'm not going to say too much about reels, simply because I don't believe they are especially important. I have indulged in expensive imported rods because I feel they give me something of an edge and are such a pleasure to cast. I use mid-priced reels – and even these are probably better than I truly need. If a reel holds your fly line plus about 80 yards of backing (half that amount would be ample for river fishing), and is free running with a click drag, then it will do the job just fine.

What about these wonderful disc drags we keep hearing about, I hear you ask? The reels I use – the Orvis Battenkill range – do happen to have a disc drag, but I *never* use the drag to fight a fish. Here's why. Say you hook a sleek 7-pound torpedo of a rainbow that decides to rocket away on a long run. In a few seconds, all your fly line will be off the reel, and you are into your backing. You have set your drag at medium to exert steady pressure. As the fish runs, the backing is coming off a smaller diameter of the spindle, so the drag exerts a much greater pressure on the line. You try to fiddle around with the control on the back of the reel to slacken off the drag – but everything happens so fast there is no time to make the correct adjustment. The result, with too much resistance from the reel plus all that fly line slicing through the water, is usually saying goodbye to that big fish. Either the hook will pull out, or the tippet will break.

I set my disc drag on light – and play all my fish by palming or fingering the spool rim. You can get exactly the same effect with the much cheaper click drag reels.

The new large arbour reels are all the rage overseas – particularly in the UK reservoir scene. The large-diameter spool means that you *can* play a fish using the disc drag – if you really feel the need to. Another advantage is that the large spool reduces line 'memory', causing less of those nasty coils that tangle when you shoot line. Of course, line retrieve is also faster with the big spool. Most of the large arbour reels are designed for 6- or 7-weight rods and up, making them too heavy for the 4-and 5-weight outfits popular here.

I can only find one suitable ultra-lightweight large arbour on the market at the moment. Manufactured by Loop, it costs an arm and a leg – so far I have resisted the temptation!

LINES

Unlike reels, for goodness sake, don't skimp on fly lines. Choosing a quality line is every bit as vital as choosing a decent rod. A poorly designed, cheap line will frustrate your best attempts at casting, and probably lie in annoying zigzags on the water.

Equally disappointing are floating lines that sink – the tip section is especially prone to this – and sinking lines that insist on floating. Well-designed lines are the result of years of research by the manufacturers. They turn over long

leaders with ease, have little 'memory' (those annoying coils and zigzags), and a slick finish that shoots like a dream.

Your first purchase should be a **floating line**. Avoid the brightly coloured lines, especially orange, and go for white, cream or, better still, grey or brown. A strike indicator is a far more efficient way of detecting takes than a gaudy orange line, and much less likely to scare off the fish.

Intermediate and sinking lines should be in earthy colours – fawn, brown or green. Clear intermediates have also been around for several years. The theory is that, being translucent, they are less visible to fish. Sounds okay, but I have noticed that clear lines shine, and give off a lot of flash on sunny days.

I have been switching between clear intermediates and the standard amber version for the past five years, and I can't detect the slightest difference in catches between the two. I will say, though, that the clear lines cast very well and shoot like a rocket, so there is certainly a plus on that side.

By the way, lines are graded according to the weight of the first 30 feet of line measured in grains (known as the AFTM system). Thus, you would think that all 5-weight lines, for example, would have the same casting 'feel'. Probably due to differences in taper design, this is certainly not the case. And I also suspect that there might be some leeway in the way in which line manufacturers weigh that first 30 feet.

It is very important to try out a line before you buy it. You might find that the ideal line for your rod and casting style

The casting performance of the latest graphite rods and modern hi-tech lines is outstanding. A couple of spare reel spools are useful to allow a quick change in line sinking rates.

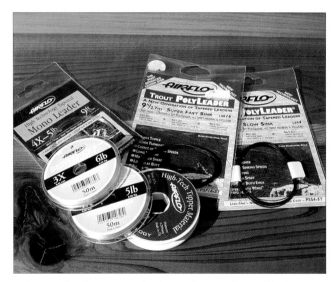

Likewise, developments in leaders and tippets have added new dimensions to fly-fishing. Among the most useful are the versatile sinking leader systems and fluorocarbon tippet material.

Roger Baert holds a brown trout for the camera, immediately prior to release. This particular dam has extensive weed growth and produces sizable fish. We don't mess around with light tippets here – 2×, or heavier, is essential to bully a big trout out of trouble.

could be one line weight lighter or heavier than your rod rating, depending on the make and model of line.

Lastly, many lines are specific to river or stillwater use, so we will revisit this topic later in the book. Generally speaking, though, I prefer weight-forward lines to gain a bit of distance on still water, and double tapers for all my river fishing.

LEADERS

Leader performance is vitally important to allow the smooth transfer of energy from the (thick) fly line to the (much finer) tippet, and hence the fly. Thus, all standard leaders are tapered to give good 'turnover'. In the past, most anglers simply made up their own leaders by knotting together lengths of nylon monofilament, gradually stepping down in thickness. You can still do this if you wish, but manufactured tapered leaders are much easier to use, and all the knots in the old home-made leaders tended to pick up weed and other muck.

There are also the new **sinking leader** systems, such as Airflow Polyleaders. Modern sinking leaders don't just serve to turn over the fly – they also perform the very useful function of controlling fishing depth. These are covered

in more detail in the stillwater section, along with **fluorocarbon tapered leaders**.

TIPPET

Tippet material is also really important stuff. It serves as the last link between the leader and fly, and therefore affects leader turnover, fly presentation (mobility) and, of course, your ability to actually land that big trout.

Trout tend to be unpredictable in their reaction to tippet. You could fish an extremely heavy tippet at all times and lose very few trout, but you may also hook very few. I have had countless experiences where fish attempt to eat my strike indicator – attached to the thickest part of the leader (probably 30-pound breaking strain!). On other days, especially on dams with lots of fishing pressure, they shy away from even the finest hi-tech tippet.

When you buy a spool of tippet, it is graded by diameter (the old '×' system dating right back to the days of gut 'cast', as they called it then). You will notice that different brands of tippet vary greatly in stated breaking strain. A 4× tippet might be quoted as having anything from a 3- to a 6-pound breaking strain.

A well-stocked dry-fly box. To avoid crushing the delicate hackles on a dry fly, a box with compartments is best. The expensive aluminum fly boxes look stylish, but a cheap, clear plastic box will do the job just as well.

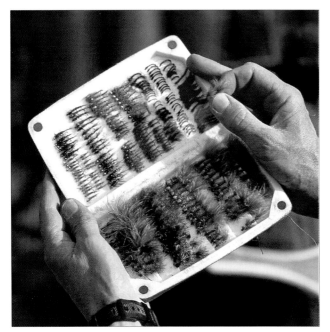

Foam boxes are absolutely fine for nymphs and streamer patterns. And foam fly boxes float – an important bonus when wading or float tubing.

Common sense will tell you that the 6-pound 4× tippet is the better choice, but I'm afraid it is not that simple!

The very thin tippet materials often have a high breaking strain under *gradual* load. If you tie a piece of that 4× tippet to a spring balance and steadily increase the load it will probably break at around 6 pounds. However, if you jerk sharply, it might break as easily as a length of cotton.

Many '**ultra-strong**' **tippet** materials have very low shock resistance. Often these tippets also have poor abrasion tolerance – so if a trout runs you across rocks or even just weed, you can get broken off very easily. I have not only lost a lot of fish on the 'ultra-strong' materials, but have also been smashed on the take many times without even striking.

A practical tippet material needs good shock and abrasion resistance, and should also be as fine as possible for its (quoted) breaking strain. Therefore, the 'high-strength' nylons are not necessarily the best choice.

These days, I fish **fluorocarbon tippet** a lot more than **nylon**. I will go into the pros and cons of this excellent (albeit expensive) material in the stillwater section.

A last word on tippet for the moment then. If you are looking for a very cheap, reliable tippet, then good old Maxima nylon monofilament – favoured by spin-fishers – takes some beating. It is a bit on the thick and wiry side, but it is as tough as old boots.

FLIES

Tie or buy?

Just about everyone buys flies when they first take up trout fishing. After a while, though, the question arises – should I start tying my own? My answer would be a qualified 'Yes!' But you need to make this decision for the right reasons.

If you are doing it just to save money then forget it. Fly-tying becomes an addiction, just like fishing, and I don't know any tier who can resist collecting materials – including all the obscure stuff that you are *sure* you will find a use for, but somehow never do.

The *right* reason for going the 'roll-your-own' route, is that you will get exactly the patterns you want, tied on the very best quality hooks (which, of course, also happen to be rather expensive). And, in the case of nymph or streamer patterns, you can add precisely the amount of weighting required for your local fishing conditions. All this adds up to flies that you are happy with and can fish with lots of confidence – and that is a huge factor in this game. Not to mention the fact that it feels good to have caught trout on flies that you have made personally.

And, the very act of tying is extremely satisfying and relaxing – almost akin to meditation. After a day on a big dam fighting a howling wind in a kick boat, I'm inclined to think that fly-tying may be more relaxing than actually going fishing!

Patterns

How many fly patterns do you really need to catch fish regularly? Probably a lot less than you think for South African conditions – if you choose wisely.

I don't usually analyse the number of fish I catch each year, but just for this book I did the following exercise. (By the way, I am not using the exercise to boast about the number of fish that I caught in a year, so please bear with me on this one.) My fishing log for the year 2002 shows that I went fishing 95 times (many of these were very short sessions on local waters before or after work – in case you were wondering if all I do is fish!). In total, I caught 637 trout, these in a wide range of waters, from really small streams right through to huge dams. I also counted the number of fly patterns I carry in my five large fly boxes that are crammed full to

Most fly tiers end up collecting a vast array of materials; you may not actually save money by tying your own flies, but it is a rewarding and wonderfully relaxing off-shoot of the sport.

overflowing. I have 110 patterns, many of which are tied in at least three sizes (it was pretty boring counting all that lot, I can tell you!). But now comes the interesting bit. Of the 637 trout, 618 (about 97%) were caught on just 18 patterns. All 18 patterns are included in this book (*see* pages 50–51, and 64–65) – plus a couple of extras that I would not want to be without under special conditions, such as when the trout are ultra shy, or when the water is very discoloured and a high-visibility fly is called for.

And the other 90 fly patterns that I carry? Well, I like to experiment – especially when it comes to the latest American and British developments. You never know when something new and devastatingly effective will appear on the scene.

Most of the time, though, 20 or so diverse and well-chosen fly patterns are sufficient to catch plenty of trout on any South African river or dam.

You will notice my fly selection in this book does not include many of the local 'old favourites' such as the Mrs Simpson, Hamill's Killer, Walker's Killer, Red Setter, and so on. This is not because they are not good patterns – they are, and must have caught thousands of South African trout over the years. It's just that I believe many of the modern patterns are generally better and, on occasion, hugely more effective than the old standards.

Oh yes, and you are going to need boxes for those flies. I find the floating foam boxes to be the most practical for all nymphs and streamers. And for dry flies, you'll need a box with compartments to prevent the hackles from becoming crushed. The cheap, clear plastic boxes are fine. Aluminum dry-fly boxes made by the likes of Wheatley in England are considered very classy, but the cost is horrendous. I'm glad I bought my Wheatley dry-fly box 25 years ago! By the way, the aluminium boxes don't float, so try not to drop them when kick boating or wading a river!

NETS

If you are planning to release most of your trout – and I hope you are – then a soft mesh net is essential. Those cheap old hard nylon knotted mesh nets will rip fins and scrape off scales, so if you are still using one, please get rid of it. You don't necessarily need to ditch the net frame, just fit a new soft net bag. A friend recently converted his old knotted net into an excellent home-made version. He told me that the soft black mesh he employed is used in the manufacture of ladies' bras – I would imagine rather racy ones at that! I did not have the heart to ask how he actually got hold of the stuff. However, it did make an excellent soft net and, I imagine, one that the trout will also appreciate!

Net frames are constructed from either metal or wood. Metal is cheaper, but if you are kick boating, then you will need to arrange some kind of leash for the net. Otherwise, sooner or later, your net is sure to disappear into that gaping void into which all sinking objects dropped from a kick boat eventually go. By the way, McLean have a 'weigh-and-release' net with a built-in spring balance – rather handy.

The hoop-style wooden net frames are very much in vogue. I have to admit that they look stylish, and more importantly, they *float*. Locally manufactured wood hoop nets have recently become available, so it is now unnecessary

Soft mesh nets are essential to avoid damaging fish. After I took a quick snap, this pretty 4-pound brown swam off strongly. I hope to meet this fish again in a few years' time, when it will have more than doubled in size!

Neoprene chest waders provide the most effective protection against the winter chill. The water temperature on this particular day was a mere 8°C. Generally, I prefer greens and browns for fly-fishing attire. Trout are less likely to see you if you blend in with the surroundings.

to pay the ridiculously inflated prices charged for imported models. I carry a medium-sized wood hoop net when fishing rivers. For still waters, I use a large 'steelhead'-sized wood hoop net – you never know when you are going to latch onto a very big trout when dam fishing.

CLOTHING AND WADERS

First and foremost, fly-fishing clothing should protect you from the vicious South African sun (UV levels are ridiculously high in the trout high grounds), wind, cold and rain. It is also important to blend in with your surroundings, so that you don't scare the wits out of the ever-watchful trout. You can either try to look like a bush and go for greens and browns, or you can pretend to be a piece of sky and wear pale grey or light blue clothing. Trying to look like a bush works best for me, so my fishing shirts (long sleeved for sun protection), sweater and jacket are all in dull greens and browns.

Fly-fishing waistcoats with a multitude of tackle pockets are popular. However, I find them very hot in summer, and prefer to carry gear, food and water in a small shoulder bag. On longer hikes, I use a light day-backpack. A hat is essential –

not only to keep off the sun, but also to shade your eyes when trying to spot fish. I prefer a wide-brimmed leather hat. Nicely worn and tatty clothing is considered very cool among seasoned fly-fishers; at all costs, avoid wearing stuff that looks new. Other anglers will pick up on this and say, '*Aha* – novice!'

Neoprene chest waders are the choice of most local fly-anglers. They keep you warm in winter, which is good, but are pretty hot in high summer. The new, lightweight, 'breathable' waders made from Gore-Tex™-type material are also stocked by some of the fly-fishing shops. They are, I've been told, cool in summer, but chilly in winter, and very expensive. I have yet to try them, but wonder how the thin material would fare with brambles, thorns and barbed-wire fences? During hot weather, I prefer to simply 'wet wade'. Shorts are not a good idea, as your legs get cut to shreds by brambles and thorns, and you might also find yourself covered in ticks. You can buy 'proper' fast-drying fishing trousers, although an old pair of jeans works fine.

Lastly, footwear. Cheap canvas 'desert-type' boots are light and dry out quickly. Proper hiking boots or old takkies, while okay, are rather heavy when wet.

Safety first! Before setting out, check that your float tube or kick boat is correctly inflated. Always wear a buoyancy-aid waistcoat, especially when venturing out on big waters.

FLOAT TUBES AND KICK BOATS

Most of South Africa's trout dams are in the smallish to medium-size range, and are ideally suited to float tubes and kick boats. Conventional boats tend to be noisy, cumbersome and difficult to control when wind drifting. A tube or kick boat allows perfect control of drift by finning, and is the ultimate in stealthy fishing.

Like many anglers who have been in this game for some time, I started out with the old **doughnut-style float**

tube – made from the inner tube of a truck tyre, with a webbing seat to support the angler. Doughnuts are really difficult to get into – especially as you have to put on your fins before squeezing into the tube. Entering the water requires a most undignified backwards duck waddle; falling over in the process is not unusual, and provides an endless source of amusement for your fishing buddies!

Although the later models include a second small tube as a backrest and 'emergency' floatation in case of puncture, I have never felt at ease in these contraptions. They always seem a little claustrophobic – after all, if there *is* a problem, how on earth would you get out of the thing? You can pick up a second-hand doughnut tube very cheaply these days, but unless you are seriously cash strapped, my advice would be to give them a miss.

Doughnuts have been replaced by the modern **U-shaped float tubes**. Getting in and out of the water is much easier, and certainly more dignified. Also, you don't get that trapped-in feeling, so if things do go wrong it is easy to make a fast exit.

As with rods and lines, I would strongly advise you to try before you buy. I once bought a U-tube that had a seat very low in the water and high tackle pouches, making casting very awkward. Simply put, it was horrible to fish from and I got rid of the thing after three outings. Ideally, you need to sit *just in* or *slightly above* the water.

These days, I use the **Bullfrog U-tube** for fishing small- to medium-sized dams. The seat is at a convenient height, just above water level, so chest waders are unnecessary in warm weather.

The other flotation option is the **pontoon** or **kick boat**. In this, you sit above water level, again avoiding the need for waders in hot weather. Getting in and out is even easier than a U-tube. I find pontoon boats the most comfortable to fish from, but again, you need to try one out before you make a purchase. Some have seats set far too high, so it is impossible to reach down into the water to unhook and release a fish. Others are so huge that they catch the wind like a sail. This makes it tiring to hold position by finning, requiring an anchor on a windy day – a hassle every time you want to move to another spot.

I have adapted my pontoon boat to take a battery and sneaker motor. The electric motor is completely silent, and the 55-amp/hour car battery is a spare that charges from my 4x4, so it all works very conveniently. At slow speeds, I have a range of 3 or 4 kilometres. I was the first among my group of fishing friends to go this route, and initially got comments like 'Oh Nigel, you're just being lazy using a *motor*!' However, having sneaker power is a huge advantage on the larger dams. On big water, productive areas can be widely spaced – often much too far to fin your way around to all the best spots. Just being able to sit back and glide along a 1-kilometre-long dam is a real pleasure – stopping and 'cherry picking' the best fish-holding areas as you go. Also, getting caught in a rapidly approaching storm is always a concern for tubers and fin-powered kick boaters. Now I can set my motor on high speed and zoom back to safety. And I have often towed my non-motorised float-tubing friends to safety when the weather has turned dicey. I notice the comments about 'being lazy' ceased some time ago!

Talking of safety, some kind of life jacket or buoyancy aid is an absolutely essential accessory for all tubing and kick-boat fishing. Needless to say, you should not even consider going onto the water if you can't swim, but even a good swimmer can get into difficulties. Many dams have thick weedbeds that I would not care to try to swim through without a buoyancy aid. Also, getting dumped into freezing water could trigger shock and panic. The floatation jacket I use is made locally (in Durban) by Tripper. It comes in a tasteful dark green, with fair-sized pockets, so essentially it serves as a fishing waistcoat as well as a lifejacket.

Don't take chances out there. No fish is ever worth risking your life.

OTHER STUFF

You can so easily go overboard on fly-fishing **accessories**. I prefer the minimalist approach.

The following is the stuff you *really* need. Sunscreen, polarised sunglasses, line clippers, a small pair of scissors, a hook-sharpening stone, artery forceps, fly floatant, sinking/de-greasing agent (clay mixed with washing-up liquid works fine – store it in a film cannister), deep soft weight, strike indicators (more on those later), water temperature thermometer, and a spring balance that weighs up to14 pounds (hey, let's think positive here!). That's it – anything more is, to my mind, superfluous, and you just get bogged down with so much junk that you can't find what you are looking for.

Time to go fishing …

All set for a day on a big dam. I have adapted my kick boat to take an electric trolling motor. A recent addition is a sonar fish finder – useful for locating underwater structure. Extra-large tackle pouches hold my drinking water, lunch, fly boxes and other essential 'stuff'.

CASTING

Most river fishing only requires short casts, with the emphasis on accuracy and a delicate presentation. When fishing heavy nymph rigs, use a slow casting action and make sure that the line has straightened behind you before commencing the forward stroke.

There are essentially two ways to learn how to cast – the easy way and the hard way.

Unfortunately, I learnt the hard way. That is, I taught myself – a frustrating, difficult and ultimately unsatisfactory path to have taken. And once learnt, bad casting habits are difficult to correct.

I first picked up a fly rod in the mid-1960s at the age of 12, and even after all these years of fly-fishing, I still cannot honestly say that I am a great caster. I do, occasionally, receive compliments. Some folks are kind enough to comment that my casting is 'good', or my style 'effortless'. This is more a case of knowing my own limits in terms of distance casting, so that at a glance it looks like I am doing okay. However, when I fish with truly gifted casters, I can see in an instant that I don't have the fluid ease and power of a great caster.

And many of us are introduced to the sport by a friend who does 'a bit of fly-fishing'. This is not a good plan either. Not only are you bound to pick up your friend's casting faults, you'll probably add a few of your own. In fact, this introduction to fly-fishing is possibly even worse than going the self-taught route!

Now, the easy way to learn is to get *proper* instruction from an *experienced professional casting instructor*. I cannot stress this enough. If you are new to the game, and keen to learn how to cast properly, get professional lessons *first*.

Fortunately, trout fishing rarely requires exceptional skill in distance casting. A person with reasonable coordination can often be taught to cast adequately in an hour or so. If you were fly-fishing salt water, of course, it would be different – excellent double-haul technique and 30 yards plus would be mandatory.

To be able to trout fish, I would say that about 15 yards on a windless day – in other words, half of a standard-weight forward line – would be about the minimum casting distance required to get you fishing effectively. If you can push out 20 or even 25 yards, that would be better. Not that you will need that sort of distance often, but being able to generate the line speed required for a 25-yard cast in still air means you could punch 15 yards into a moderate headwind – and that ability might come in very handy.

If you can't manage 15 yards – and this means turning over the leader properly at that distance, and not slapping the water when false casting – then you have a problem. To put it bluntly, you need guidance from a professional. Poor casting will not only limit your catches but, far more importantly, it will greatly impair your enjoyment of the entire fly-fishing experience, and you will probably return from a day on the water feeling miserable and frustrated, and seriously consider selling your fly rod and buying a set of golf clubs!

Most fly-fishing shops offer casting clinics and instruction, and many offer this service at no extra cost when you purchase a new outfit.

I believe you can learn a great deal from fly-fishing books and magazines in terms of new techniques, fishing strategies and fly patterns. It is, however, very difficult to learn the basic casting skills from a book. For this reason, I have kept this section rather short, and focused only on essential skills, plus a few tips to help you to overcome common casting problems.

THE BASIC CAST

The basic cast is the foundation for all other styles. Get this right and you are well on the way. As I am sure you know, the basic cast has two components – the **back cast** and the **forward stroke**. Each is essentially a mirror image of the other. Rod movement comes from the elbow and, to some extent, from the shoulder. Some styles use a little wrist flick at the end of each stroke to add zip to the cast, but by and large you need to retain a firm wrist.

Building power needs to be done with a smooth acceleration, and then an abrupt stop and pause. So a typical back cast would go like this: *smooth* acceleration, and a *positive* stop when the rod has reached about the 1 o'clock to 2 o'clock position. Then *pause* to allow the rolling loop to begin to straighten behind you. *Just* as the back cast is about to straighten, go into the forward stoke. Again, it is a smooth acceleration and a positive stop, this time at about the 10 o'clock position; it can be helpful to consciously squeeze the rod handle when you make the stop. Imagine you are trying to flick water from a paintbrush; you would steadily accelerate speed with your elbow, and then abruptly stop to aim the water where you want it to go. Fly-casting is the same, except you are making the build-up and stop behind you for the back cast, and then a mirror action to get the line to go forward.

Modern rods and lines are so well designed that they do most of the work for you. Casting – at least up to 15 yards or so – should be completely *effortless*. If you are finding that a lot of *oomph* is required, then concentrate on refining your technique.

HAULING FOR DISTANCE

So far, we have concentrated on the action of the rod hand. What you do with your line hand is just as important. A haul is simply pulling on the line to add momentum to the cast. This is an extremely efficient way of increasing line speed and hence distance – again, with *very little effort*. You can add a haul on either the forward or the back cast, or both – which is, of course, the famous **double-haul** technique.

Hauling has been taught in different ways over the years. The modern style uses the haul just before you stop the rod, say about $^1/_{10}$ of a second before the stop.

This is how you haul on a back cast. Pull down on the line just before you stop the rod (a 2-foot haul is good at

It is easiest to learn to cast with a 5-weight rod. The ultra-lightweights, like the 2-weight shown here, are best left until you have mastered the basics.

first) and then *immediately* take your line hand up again so that it is close to the rod. Pause to allow the line to almost straighten behind you, and then go into the forward-stroke sequence. Add the same haul near the end of the forward stroke, and you are double hauling. This will really get the line zipping through the air and will allow you to shoot a lot of the loose line coiled at your feet.

Once learned, you will probably find that you use the double haul instinctively. I tend to use a **mini-haul** (pulling the line a few inches) constantly, even when casting moderate distances. This greatly increases the efficiency of casting, and means that I don't experience the slightest tiredness in my casting arm, even when I have fished continuously for hours on end.

(a) (b) (c)

(d) (e) (f)

Casting instructor Michael Greene demonstrates the double-haul cast. (a) Pick up the line from the water. (b) A smooth acceleration on the back cast loads the rod. (c) Haul down on the line just before you make the stop. (d) Immediately take your line hand back up to the rod, and then pause to allow the line to begin to straighten behind you. (e) Start the mirror-image action with a smooth acceleration on the forward stroke. (f) Add the second haul, again, just before you make the stop; then, let go of the line and watch the cast zip into the distance! Impeccable timing is essential for an efficient double haul. I'm tempted to say, 'Don't try this at home, folks!' A good instructor will get you double hauling like a pro with a fraction of the difficulty and frustration you might experience if you attempt to teach yourself this technique.

Here is a neat little trick that will impress the heck out of your friends – and catch more trout. Pick up the line with a roll cast (top).
Go into the back-cast sequence, shooting a little line after making the stop. Add a mini-haul on the forward stroke (above). The result
is an effortless 18 yards without the need to false cast.

ROLL CASTING

There is just one other technique that I would include among essential skills and that is the roll cast. Fortunately, this is an easy one. The roll cast appears to have only a forward stroke, although you are in fact using the water to load the rod beforehand. So there *is* a back cast involved, although you are not actually throwing the line behind you, as you would in the basic cast.

Start with not more than 10 yards of line on the water in front of you. Tilt the rod back to about the 2 o'clock position, and make a smart push forward and down. This will cause a rolling loop of line to unfurl in front of you … I told you it was easy! The beauty of the roll cast is that you can get a line out when there are bushes or trees, or even a high bank directly behind you – an impossible situation for a standard basic cast. The roll cast is also a great way to pick

A 2-pound wild river brown taken on a heavily weighted nymph. To aid in the casting of this rig, I used a 5-weight line on my 4-weight rod.

up line before going into the basic-cast sequence, thus avoiding repeated false casting.

COPING WITH WIND WITHOUT GETTING A FLY STUCK IN YOUR EAR

Windy days can be a bit daunting, but there are ways to deal with any wind short of a howling gale.

Let's do the easy one first. All fly-casters are aware that a light to moderate **tail wind** can enhance distance. You can capitalise on this by putting a bit more beef into the back cast and then aiming high on the forward stroke to shoot lots of line. The line 'carries' in the wind so you get plenty of distance. In fact, this is about the only situation where I find I can easily cast my full 30-yard weight-forward line on the 5-weight outfit – but then I did warn you that I am not a great caster! Casting **into** the wind is tough. Aiming the forward cast low over the water helps, because wind velocity is slightly less at water level. Also, tight casting loops created by abbreviating the power stroke help cut though the wind, and, of course, a double haul on the line will add punch.

For a right-handed caster a **left to right crosswind** is not too bad. You might find you get a bit of drift so accuracy is not so good, but at least the wind will keep the line and fly away from your body.

A **right to left crosswind** is the nasty one with a good chance of the getting-a-fly-stuck-in-your-ear syndrome. I've only ever had this happen once, but I can assure you it has little to recommend it! If the right to left wind is light and you only need a short cast, then tilting the rod plane to about 45° should keep the line and fly away from your body.

A strong right to left wind is a problem. I find the safest option is to cast *backwards*. In other words, stand with your back to the water and cast with the rod tilted away from you a bit. It is not easy to be accurate, but at least the technique will ensure that the line is safely blown away from your body.

All of the above principles also apply to left-handed casters, but the opposite way around, of course. Eye protection is very sensible for all casting. I wear polarised sunglasses whenever I am fishing; amber lenses are best on an overcast day, otherwise things get to look a bit gloomy.

TROUBLESHOOTING
Cracking off flies
This is the result of a poorly timed cast. Use a longer pause on the back cast to allow most of the line to straighten before commencing the forward stroke.

Hitting the ground on the back cast
This is also usually a timing problem. You might be pausing too long and allowing the line to fall to the ground before starting the forward stroke. Using too wide a casting stroke – for example, letting the rod slop back to the 3 o'clock position – will cause a similar problem.

Slapping the water when false casting
I've seen folk do this on both the forward *and* back casts when float tubing. It not only looks really horrible, it also frightens the trout! Again, too wide or sloppy a casting stroke is the cause.

Trailing loops, wind knots or hitting the rod with the fly
These are all very annoying. The most common cause is applying too much power early in the casting stroke, causing the rod tip to dip and follow a concave path. Remember, use a *smooth* acceleration and then a *positive* stop in both the forward and back casts.

Leader fails to straighten
This one is not hard to fix, as long as you are not trying to cast beyond your maximum distance capability. Simply stop the line with your line hand in the shooting phase. This creates momentum in the leader, so that it continues unfurling. When casting into wind, you can add a little tug back on the line to enhance leader turnover.

A put-and-take fishery is the ideal place to learn to fly-fish. Hatchery trout are usually tolerant of the odd splashy cast, and it does not hurt to take a couple home to eat as such waters are regularly stocked with 'takeable' fish.

Trout fishing has increased greatly in popularity over the past decade, and it seems that the trend is accelerating. I am seeing a lot more anglers on my local waters now than I did even a couple of years ago. Fortunately, more trout venues are becoming available to cope with the demand.

Heavy fishing pressure can easily lead to a rapid deterioration in catches – *unless* trout waters are well managed. Broadly speaking, fishery management takes two forms. On one hand, dams or streams are stocked with trout fingerlings, or fry, which are allowed to develop naturally in their new environment. In this same category, many trout streams, and a handful of dams with good feeder streams, have wild-spawning, self-supporting populations. In both instances, fishing will invariably decline as rod pressure increases. Therefore, the harvest, or number of fish killed, has to be strictly controlled, either by setting low bag limits, or employing a catch-and-release ethic, so that the fish live long enough to grow to adult size.

André Robins holds a rare, wild-spawned stillwater brown. The stunning colours are the result of a hundred years of natural breeding in the dam's feeder stream.

Small fishing clubs can offer solitude as well as outstanding fishing. Here Roger Baert prepares for an outing on a pristine high-altitude dam, where annual membership is restricted to 10.

On the other hand, dams and streams are regularly stocked with hatchery fish that are already at a takeable size. This method of stocking is known as 'put and take'. Growth is often augmented with pellet feeding after stocking. As you can imagine, this style of management is very expensive for the fishery owner, and such waters pretty much have to run on a commercial basis; here, you may be required to pay for fish by the kilo, in addition to a daily rod fee.

Generally, anglers prefer to fish for grown-on, or wild-spawned trout – myself included – simply because the act

of catching naïve, 'tame' trout that may have been eating pellets in a hatchery a week ago, is less 'authentic'. However, I do not take an overly purist attitude towards the stocking of large fish. If that is the only fishing you have available locally, then go for it – catching 'stockies' is certainly a whole lot better than no trout fishing at all!

TROUT-FISHING VENUES

All trout waters in South Africa are privately owned. Overall, **fly-fishing clubs** undoubtedly offer the best value for money – even though you may catch mostly smaller trout. An initial deposit or joining fee is usually payable, but annual fees are low. The upside is that you can usually fish as often as you like and, in some cases, you may have a variety of 40 or more venues from which to choose. On the downside, a large membership – which allows a club to keep fees low – will usually mean that the waters get fished a lot.

Stocking is mostly done with small fish – again to keep the costs down. Many of the larger clubs still allow generous bag limits of between two and four fish per day. Although you may catch good numbers of trout from club waters, trophy-sized, grown-on fish are likely to be rare. The trout seldom stay in a dam long enough to grow very large. A notable exception is the Cape Town-based Cape Piscatorial Society, which has adopted a catch-and-release ethic on all their rivers. It would be good to see more clubs follow the CPS philosophy, and make at least some of their waters 'no kill'.

There are also the small, often informal, fishing clubs, where a group of anglers get together, rent water from a farmer and control the stocking. The advantage is that fishing pressure is kept low. Also, it is easier to obtain consensus among a small group to limit the harvest. You are, of course, going to pay more, but the best of the small clubs offer excellent fishing for big trout. Obviously, these clubs have limited membership, and there could be a long waiting list to join (although it may help if you know some of the existing members!).

Essentially, **day-fishing** waters are operated commercially, and here you will pay a daily rod fee. Day waters vary from pure put-and-take, to authentic grown-on, or truly wild trout waters. The quality of fishing can vary enormously depending on stocking policy, rod pressure, and how effectively it is managed. Fly-fishing shops in the area will be able to offer up-to-date advice on where to find good day-fishing venues. An increasingly popular trend is the 'rent the cottage and get the fishing thrown in for free' type of arrangement. Often, no day-fishing is allowed, so you have to rent accommodation in order to have access to these

Many trout-fishing venues also conveniently offer accommodation. Tillietudlem, on the Upper Dargle in KwaZulu-Natal, is a good example, where visitors have access to several dams as well as to the headwaters of the Elands River.

waters. This makes a good holiday break a couple of times a year, but for local anglers wanting to fish regularly, the cost can be prohibitive.

Price-wise, **fishing syndicates** are at the top end of the scale. Essentially, you have to purchase a share in a farm, and it is very much a case of 'buyer beware'. The very best syndicate waters can be outstanding; others are little more than glorified holiday timeshare – with a bit of trout fishing thrown in. Before making this kind of investment, it would be wise to try out the fishing. Find out how much rod pressure the farm endures, and check on the stocking policy.

As I said, though, the best syndicate waters offer wonderful fishing … I often drive past some very famous syndicate dams in the Dargle area (on my way to rather less exclusive fishing), and I always cast an envious eye at these waters and think, 'Hey, I just wish I could afford it!'

And now we come to the **private waters**, 'secret' places behind locked gates that only a select few are allowed to fish.

Where, to quote John Gierach, 'all the trout are as long as your leg.' Of course, not all private waters are like this. I have had some days on private dams where I haven't seen even a sign of a fish. However, the best of it can be so good it could spoil you for life!

The problem lies in getting into these places. A polite enquiry to the owner seldom works these days, as so many anglers will have tried this before. Entry is usually by invitation only, but it might help if you know someone who is a friend of the owner. And there is a certain protocol involved; you should offer to release all the fish you catch (although the owner might ask you to keep a fish for him).

Also, don't push your luck! I have a lot of local contacts, so I get to fish some very private places, but I only ask to visit each of these waters a few times each season.

When water temperatures are favourable, a cast back towards bank-side reeds and weedbeds usually results in action. An experienced angler has a 'nose' for these areas, and I noticed that Michael Greene, on his first visit to Drayton Dam, made straight for this productive spot.

'HEY, WHAT FLY ARE YOU USING?'

This has to be the most commonly asked question when you are successfully getting into the fish.

Certainly, there will be days when the fish are very fussy, but for most of the time, South African trout are not particularly fly selective, so I would put fly patterns way down on the list of priorities.

In still waters, your main aim should be to *find* the fish. As a rule of thumb, 70% of the fish are likely to be found in less than 30% of a dam's surface area. Clearly, if you fish a dam randomly, much of the time your fly will not even be within sight of a trout. Locating these hot spots – and they can vary greatly at different times of the year, or even hours of the day – is the first step towards a good catch.

Presentation is the next priority. This means finding the correct feeding depth and using the appropriate retrieve for the trout's current mood.

So, if you meet someone on the dam who is catching loads of fish, a more useful line of questioning would be: '*Where* are you getting them?' 'How *deep* are you fishing?'

'*What* retrieve are you using?' And, finally, 'Oh yes, and which fly is working?'

LOCATING TROUT – THE KEY TO SUCCESS THROUGH THE SEASONS

The needs of trout are fairly simple. They need food, of course. Security from predators – such as otters and white-breasted cormorants, and, in the case of heavily fished waters, from the likes of you and me, the human predators – is very important. Trout also need comfortable water temperatures with sufficiently oxygenated water.

The relative importance of these factors varies with the seasons. For example, in high summer, the shallows may be packed with juicy dragonfly and damsel nymphs, but by mid-morning, high water temperatures and accompanying poor oxygen levels may see the trout vacating these food larders for deeper, cooler water, even though it means they will go hungry.

There is an additional factor that greatly influences trout location, and that is sex. Fortunately, this extra little complication only features in the equation for a short part of the year, so I will cover that in the section on winter fishing (*see* page 32).

The most important word on locating stillwater trout, no matter what the season, is always be on the lookout for visible signs of fish. In clear waters, the most effective way to spot cruising fish is through polarised lenses. Rises are, of course, a dead giveaway. Less easy to detect are the subsurface boils or swirls of nymph-feeding fish. In a rippled surface, they appear as a slight flattening of the wave pattern – easy to miss unless you know what you are looking for.

And how do you get good at spotting such fish activity? Well, that's easy – you just need to spend lots and lots of time fishing!

Spring to early summer

Generally, the most productive time of the year for trout fishing is spring to early summer. Seasons vary with altitude, but the period we are looking at is roughly early September to about early December. This is prime time, and in a normal year you can expect water temperatures to be within the trout's optimum comfort and activity zone – say about 12–18°C.

During this period, food and security are the prime indicators to locating trout, so the key to finding stillwater trout would be to look for **structure**.

Permanent structure can be broadly defined as the *physical* features that you find in the dam, for example, weedbeds, reedbeds, banks, etc. At this time of year, I head for weed. I know many anglers hate the stuff – it *is* annoying, as it gets caught up on your fly and you can very easily lose a trout in it as well. But weed means lots of food – damselfly, dragonfly and mayfly nymphs, and maybe minnow shoals as well. Weed is also an excellent place to hide if you happen to be a trout being chased by a cormorant or an otter. All of which makes for happy, well-fed, secure trout.

Unlike bass, our quarry doesn't like hiding away in heavy dense mats of weed growing right to the surface. Trout prefer the *edge* of a weedbed, along which they can patrol. This means fishing along the bank margin of weed just at the drop-off point.

Isolated weed patches far out into the dam are also a sure bet, but once again, concentrate on the *edges* of the weedbeds. Best of all would be the original feeder stream channel, if the adjacent margins are well weeded. In fact, this is the first place I head for on a dam that I haven't fished before. Also, many small- to medium-sized waters have a very fruitful area in the old stream channel about a third of the way into the main part of the dam. (By the way, this is a hot tip, as I have seldom known it to fail!)

Reedy margins can also be good on some dams. And while large browns sometimes hold up in cover of sunken trees and the like, such places are a better bet if you are after bass. For trout, always try the weed edges and channels first.

During spring, the best fishing will be in waters between 3 and 12 feet deep. In the early and later part of the day, chances are that you will find more trout in the very shallow, 3-foot-deep water. From mid-morning until about 3 pm, trout may move out into slightly deeper water, so at midday,

Decisions, decisions! As a broad rule, larger fly patterns in the size 8 to 10 range are most effective in spring and early summer, when the mature nymphs of many aquatic insects hatch.

When photographing your catch it is wise to hold the fish over water – to avoid damage should it slip from your hands. You might miss the photo opportunity, but at least the trout will be unharmed.

I think you would do best to concentrate your efforts in 6–12 feet of water.

Daytime movement can be greatly affected by **transitory structure**. A good example of transitory structure is wind. Wind creates waves, and wave action makes trout less visible, and therefore more secure from predators. On a windy day, then, trout are more likely to remain in the shallows.

On the windward bank, you may also find an area of discoloured water from the waves pounding the bank – more transitory structure. Fishing right in the discoloured water can be worthwhile. Often, though, the hot area is, again, the *edge* of the dirty water – where it mixes with clear depths of the dam. I think it is safe to say that trout have a thing about edges when it comes to structure of any form!

Cloud cover also gives trout a sense of security, and in low light conditions, they may stay active in weedy shallows right through the day. When the sun is shining, a bank shaded by trees or even a steep hillside will provide transitory structure, as fish may remain in such areas for much longer than in brightly lit shallows.

A lot of folks think that deep water must always hold the biggest fish, but this is rarely the case at this time of the year.

In fact, during the spring season, the very deep water off the dam wall is the last area I would be inclined to fish. If the depth exceeds 15 feet, the bottom is likely to be devoid of weed cover, and thus will be rather sterile in terms of trout food.

To sum up: when the water temperatures are comfortable, a trout's priority is to find lots of food in an area offering security from predators. The weed-free depths usually offer neither, so although there may be a few trout down there, most of the fish – including the big ones – are likely to be elsewhere in the shallower, more fertile feeding areas.

Mid- to late summer

In the mid- to late summer period, things get a lot tougher for both the angler and the trout. Again, altitude will influence the seasons, but you can expect the summer doldrums to last from mid-December through to sometime in March. This is the time when many of our dams unfortunately become marginal habitat for trout. Water temperatures will be in the low 20s most of the time, with peaks during a long hot spell of 24 or 25°C (a trout's maximum temperature tolerance is around 27°C, but they can only withstand this kind of heat for short periods). Warm water is low in dissolved oxygen, which can badly stress trout. Their main priority will be to find cooler,

The water clarity of this small dam is astounding. With polarised sunglasses, you can spot trout cruising 6 feet or more below the surface. Keep low, and use a stealthy approach under such conditions. It is also a good idea to wear clothing that blends in with the vegetation.

oxygen-rich water within their comfort zone – even if this means having to make the trade-off of getting less to eat and running a greater risk of predation.

At this time, a fishing thermometer can be your best tool for locating trout. In fact, during midsummer, the trout hot spots will be the cool areas. If a dam has a strong feeder stream inlet, this will invariably attract a number of fish. While the main part of the dam may be at 21 or 22°C, it is not unusual to find that the feeder stream is pouring in water that is three or four degrees cooler. The fish may be right at the stream inlet, or even in the stream itself, if it has sufficient depth. On other occasions, a little more detective work may be required.

If you are using a kick boat, you will be able the follow the cool water flow out into the dam by checking your thermometer every few metres.

I recall a short stay at Wolf Avnis' Giant's Cup Dam back in the summer of '99. Giant's Cup is a sizeable impoundment of some 25 hectares (this was my first time at this venue, so the vast expanse of water was a little daunting). Now, on big dams, the biggest challenge is to find the trout. A water-temperature reading at the dam wall showed 21°C – warmer than I would have liked to see at a high-altitude dam in December. The first evening was slow, and I only picked up one rainbow of 2 pounds. The following morning, I headed up to the top end of the dam, and fished the feeder stream inlet from my kick boat. The water temp in the stream was a mere 16°C. There had been a lot of rain over the previous few days, and the feeder stream was really pumping. I fished through the cool water, convinced this was where the fish would be – but nothing, not even a touch. It was only when I followed the stream flow almost 100 metres out into the dam that I found the action. The water here was 18°C. The trout were holding right where the cold stream water was mixing with the tepid dam. I released 10 rainbows in just a couple of hours.

I have since encountered similar situations in several other dams. It seems that very cold water may be too much of a shock to trout after a hot spell, so they prefer to hold on the edge of the cold water. Yet again, we are looking at transitory structure, and those 'edges' – in this case the edge to a temperature gradient.

If the dam you are fishing does not have a sizeable feeder stream, then midsummer location can be more difficult. Trout *may* hold in the deepest part of the dam – the same area I advised you to ignore during spring. Deep water can be cooler, and you can check this by dropping your water thermometer down into the depths on a long piece of string

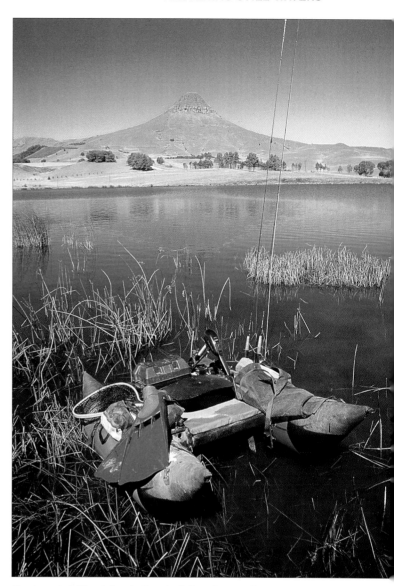

During a brief lunch break, I noticed that these reed margins were teeming with small adult grey caddis. A size 16 Elk Hair Caddis proved very effective during the afternoon rise.

(just remember to hang onto the other end, or at least tie it onto your kick boat!). At times you may record a temperature difference of two or three degrees.

The reason I said the trout *may* be down there, is that very deep water receives little light, and will not support oxygen-providing weeds. Although temperatures may be comfortable for the trout, there may be insufficient dissolved oxygen right on the bottom in 25 feet or more of water. In such cases, you may need to experiment with fishing various depths – starting right on the bottom and working your way up – to find the trout's comfort zone. At times you may find fish holding at, say, 15 feet, in 25-foot-deep water.

Weather and the time of day also greatly influence midsummer trout activity. I am fortunate in that I live close to a lot of good trout water. This means I can get a useful fix on local weather conditions. Long, hot spells mean lethargic trout. I try to avoid planning a trip at such times. Apart from lousy fishing, I know the water temperatures will be too high to safely release fish (catch and release is not successful above 21°C – but we will look at this in more detail in the Catch and Release chapter on page 69). I time my summer fishing to follow several days of cool, windy weather; if there have been a few good heavy thunderstorms to cool and oxygenate the water, so much the better. When water temperatures have dropped to the 18 or 19°C mark, you can generally expect some good fishing.

During mid- and late summer, early mornings are usually the most productive. Unfortunately, this means setting your alarm clock to go off at an unearthly hour as, ideally, you need to be on the water just before dawn. On cool, overcast, windy days, you might get lucky and find that feeding activity continues right through the day. However, if you hit a hot, sunny, flat, calm morning, it is not unusual to find that the bite stops dead by 7 am.

Autumn

As autumn approaches, things liven up considerably. In trout terms, the autumn season gets going sometime between late March and the end of April. A lot depends on how long and hot the summer has been, and on the altitude of the dam.

A pair of browns holding in cool water at a stream inlet. During very hot spells, these trout are likely to become heat stressed, and are best left alone if you intend to release your catch.

The summer of 2002/3 was a horror, with my local dams staying warm right up until the very end of April.

You can tell when the autumn fishing starts to kick in, as it corresponds with water temperatures dropping to the 16 or 17°C mark. In many ways, this season mirrors spring, when trout move to the shallow and mid-depth areas of the dam. Feeding activity often continues right through the day – especially if you have overcast, drizzly conditions, and a steady breeze to ruffle the surface (trout fishermen just love what 'normal' folks would consider to be rotten weather!).

The main difference between spring and autumn fishing revolves around the size of the trout's food – that is, the insect life, which tends to be smaller in autumn, as the mature nymph stages of many insect species have already hatched during the warmer months. Many of the dams I fish in spring with size 8 or 10 flies tend to produce best at this time of the year with size 12 or 14.

Fortunately, the weedbeds start to die back by early May, which means there is a better chance of landing a big fish on smaller hooks. In dams that carry a good minnow population, there can be an autumn fry-feeding bonanza, so be sure to carry some streamer patterns as well as small insect imitations.

Apart from the good fishing, autumn weather is generally stable, and there is less chance of getting chased off the water by a thunderstorm, which is so often the case in spring and summer. Unfortunately, this brief but wonderful season comes to an end by early June, when we head into winter.

Winter

Our June to August winter season can be patchy. I have had absolutely brilliant fishing during this period, and I have had freezing, miserable days without so much as a bite. Once water temperatures drop below 15°C, then something new begins to preoccupy our quarry – the urge to breed. The trout's driving instinct is to find running water in which to spawn over clean gravel. Feeder streams, even those that are little more than a trickle, are a big attraction. If the stream is too small and shallow for trout to ascend, they tend to mill around the inlet area. The urge to seek out such areas is so strong that it is sometimes possible to take quite a number of fish before they spook and move elsewhere. In the very rare case of dams that are fed by a sizeable river, trout may make a spawning run up the watercourse, leaving the dam virtually empty of fish (so it might be a good idea to give natural spawning dams a miss during midwinter!).

Not all trout are preoccupied with spawning activity in midwinter. I got stuck into several lively winter rainbows at Springholm Dam by fishing the weedy shallows. A weak July sun had warmed this area of the dam, so the trout were actively hunting down midge pupae.

A far more common scenario (where a good inflow is lacking) is where trout attempt to spawn over the gravel or shale margins of the dam itself. Spawning in still water is rarely successful; nonetheless, the trout go through the motions. You might find such areas along the dam wall or in places where a steep bank has eroded to form a gravel or shale margin. Once you locate these spawning areas, some very exciting close-range sight-fishing is possible. The techniques for fishing winter spawners are quite specialised, and we will take a closer look at these methods later in this chapter (*see* page 47).

To get back to finding winter fish, I must say that without a feeder stream or gravel patches, it can be a long, tough slog. Winter insect hatches are few and far between, so few fish will be rising to give an indication of their whereabouts.

You can get lucky in midwinter, though. Unseasonably warm, calm days occasionally trigger good insect hatches – usually midge, micro caddis or sometimes mayfly. This may see some nice action, with small dry flies and nymphs in the shallows, especially if the air temperature stays mild through until the evening. And if you do get lucky, make the most of it!

Generally, I do best fishing the same areas that are productive during spring and autumn. The weedbeds will mostly have died away, but other structure such as drop-offs and channels are worth a try. Usually, though, it is a case of slow, deep, patient fishing, but sooner or later something will happen.

Winter feeding activity generally peaks between 11 am and 2 pm (a civilised time of day, thank goodness – one that precludes having to get to the water at dawn, and fishing in a heavy frost with the line freezing to the rod guides!).

To sum up, stillwater trout *generally* feed in two zones: either within 2 or 3 feet from the bottom, or a similar distance from the surface. Only on rare occasions (such as a migration of midge pupae prior to hatching) will trout actively seek food in mid-water. So, you are probably going to have the best success by fishing either fairly close to the bottom, or close to or on the surface.

PRESENTATION

Once we have located the trout, the next priority is presenting the fly at the correct depth and with the appropriate retrieve.

Floating-line techniques

I'm going to begin with techniques for a floating line. It's a good place to start because floating lines are the nicest to use. They pick up cleanly from the water and cast easily. Floating lines are also the most versatile, as you can fish anywhere from the surface to pretty deep (I'll get to the deep techniques in a moment).

Fishing with a **dry fly** is the most straightforward floating line technique. I prefer a tapered nylon monofilament leader of about 8 feet, with around 3 or 4 feet of tippet – also nylon. You will notice throughout this book that I go big on fluorocarbon tippets, but not for dry fly on stillwaters. Fluorocarbon is denser than mono, so it is not a good choice when you want to float a dry fly for long periods.

Fluorocarbon will tend to drag the fly down as it sinks. Apply fly floatant to the mono leader and tippet up to about 1 foot from the fly. You will need to apply floatant to the fly as well, of course, but try to avoid getting any on that last foot of tippet. First prize is to get the last foot of tippet to sink – tippet floating in the surface film is very visible and will often put off a wary fish. If that last piece of tippet simply refuses to sink, try a de-greasing agent. The rather disgusting concoction of Fuller's Earth (or even clay or mud), mixed with washing-up liquid, works better for me than any of the shop-bought sinking agents.

Dry-fly fishing is at its most exciting when there is a good insect hatch, when you can cast to visibly rising fish. Stillwater trout are mostly cruisers, so you will need to 'lead' a fish by casting ahead of its cruising path. This is easy when a trout is rising steadily in a clear line – just place your fly 10–20 feet ahead of the last rise.

When only random rises occur across a calm dam, leading the fish will be mainly a matter of luck. Place the fly to one or other side of the rise – and just hope you guessed correctly! In a steady breeze, the fish tend to cruise the surface upwind (and make the return trip back down the dam, swimming deeper), so in a ripple it is usually a good bet to place your dry well upwind of the last rise.

Often, of course, there is very little visible surface activity. Under these circumstances, prospecting blind with a dry fly can work well – at least on some dams, and particularly in heavily stocked or less fertile waters, where trout need to watch the surface for stray terrestrial insects to supplement their diet.

Prospecting blind occasionally beats prospecting with a sunken fly hands down! For blind fishing, I like to use two dries fished in tandem for maximum attraction. A large DDD or Parachute Hopper pattern that is very visible from deep

When no fish are rising, a large attractor dry fly such as this Humpy, may draw a trout up from the depths.

down, and a small black DDD, Elk Hair Caddis or CDC Midge imitation, fished on about 4 feet of tippet tied onto the bend of the larger fly, usually does the trick. Often, a fish is brought up from the depths by the big fly, has second thoughts about it and takes the smaller pattern floating close by. This 'New Zealand-style' **two-fly rig** is one that you are going to see a lot of in the following pages. It has great advantages over the older method of fishing a dropper of about 5 inches of line created by tying a Barrel or Water Knot in the tippet. With the top fly tied onto the end of the dropper, the old rig was always prone to casting tangles – and in any case, the dropper often twisted around the tippet, giving a poor presentation.

A couple more points while we are on the subject of stillwater dry-fly fishing. Firstly, it is generally best to cast and leave the fly drifting with no movement. You only need to gradually take up slack line to keep in contact with the fly. Try to avoid fishing a dry across a strong crosswind. The belly formed in the line will cause the fly to drag unnaturally across the surface. This is where float tubers and kick boaters have a great advantage, as you can almost always position the craft so that you can fish downwind, thus avoiding drag.

Once in a while, twitching the fly, or even giving a jerky hand-twist retrieve, will induce a take. So, if nothing is happening, it is worth giving the fly a gentle pull every now and again. Don't overdo the movement, though. On very hard-fished waters, the trout will have seen this many times before, and movement on a dry fly may spook them.

Lastly, timing the strike on a dry is very different from any of the following sunk-fly techniques. Striking as soon as you detect the take is a good idea with a sunk fly. With a dry

The rise to a large fly is often aggressive. Avoid the temptation to strike instantly – allow the fish to turn with the fly first.

Wait for it … then tighten gently. The trout may be moving at speed, so use the slip strike technique to avoid smashing your tippet.

fly, it is usually essential to *delay* the strike a little, as the fish needs a moment to turn and inhale the fly. Generally, the larger the fly – and the fish – the longer the delay. If I am using a big size 8 hopper pattern, I may wait up to 3 seconds before tightening onto the fish. With a tiny fly – say a size 20 midge imitation – a 1-second delay will do the job.

The basic technique for fishing a **sunk fly** with a floating line is also pretty straightforward, but let's deal with the leader and tippet configuration first. After messing around with various leader rigs for decades, I now use only a tapered fluorocarbon leader and fluorocarbon tippet for this technique. Why fluorocarbon? Several reasons.

One, it has excellent abrasion resistance, so if a big fish takes you through weed or even over sunken branches or rocks, there is still a fair chance of landing it.

Second, fluorocarbon has great shock resistance, so fewer trout and flies are lost on 'smash takes'. The stuff is denser than water, so it sinks nicely. Also, you can straighten out kinks in the leader and tippet very easily; one good pull sorts it out, unlike nylon, which can be a real pig to straighten once it gets kinks or coils.

And, lastly, the refractive index of fluorocarbon is close to that of water, making it less visible. Some folks claim that fluorocarbon is invisible to fish. I think this is nonsense – all you have to do is put a piece of tippet in a glass of water to see that you *can* see it. Certainly, though, most makes of fluorocarbon are less visible than other tippet and leader materials of similar diameter, and that, plus all the above, is more than enough to convince me to pay the extra price for this material.

Floating-line fishing is generally associated with working the shallows up to about 5 feet. I like a 7½-foot tapered 2× fluorocarbon leader cut down to around 6 feet (chop out more from the thick end and a bit less from the thin end, to retain the steepest part of the taper). Attach 6 feet of tippet (2× or 3× fluorocarbon), using a loop-to-loop connection. Good searching patterns for the shallows are lightly weighted damsel and dragon imitations, or that perennial winner, the Woolly Bugger.

I fish only a single fly in heavy weed or snags. In all other conditions, I knot 6 feet of tippet – 1× lighter than the first lot – to the bend of the first fly, and fish a smaller, unweighted pattern on the point (that New Zealand style again!). Favourites for the point fly are the Holographic Hare's Ear, San Juan Worm, or a midge pupa imitation.

If you have been paying attention and doing your mental arithmatic, you will notice that the total leader length is now 18 feet. '*What?*' I hear you say. 'How on earth do you cast such a long leader?!' It takes a little practice, but by overpowering the cast slightly and then checking the line at the end of the shoot, it is not difficult to get a clean, straight leader turnover. Fly lines and even leaders can, and often do, spook fish in shallow water, so it's worth taking the trouble to learn to fish a long tippet. Fishing the two flies 6 feet apart has the advantage of a fish not seeing two flies moving unnaturally in tandem, and this certainly improves catches on hard-fished water. This has been proven time and again by UK competition fly-fishers, who fish flies up to 10 feet apart when the going gets tough. Also, if you miss a take on the top fly, you are less likely to foul-hook the fish on the point fly with a long trail between the two – largely overcoming the foul hooking problem associated with two-fly rigs. I know we all want to catch fish, but preferably not by snagging them across the back!

Try to minimise false casting when fishing the shallows. In calm conditions and crystal-clear water, a fly line flashing overhead can frighten a lot of fish. Always watch the tip of the fly line and leader as the fly sinks. A dart forward or drawing of the line means you have a take 'on the drop'. Often, you won't feel a take as the fly sinks, so it is essential to strike on any visual indication. Strike quickly, as trout sometimes spit out the fly within a second or two. Once you begin the retrieve, takes in shallow water are usually felt very positively on the line, leaving you in no doubt as to when to strike.

Much the same leader setup is used for **deep nymphing** with a floating line. I like a fairly heavily weighted top fly to get depth quickly. The point fly remains unweighted, and is attached by the same 6 feet of finer tippet. The inherent problem with deep nymphing with a floating line is that when you allow the flies to sink way down, the leader hangs down at almost right angles to the line. This 'hinge' means that you will seldom feel a take on the line, even when retrieving. You may detect some hits by carefully watching

the tip of the floating line, but this becomes difficult if there is any kind of ripple on the water.

A yarn indicator knotted onto the leader about 4 inches from the end of the fly line solves all the problems of bite detection. Adding the strike indicator makes this an incredibly sensitive rig. Over in England, they call it 'Fishing the Bung', and the tactic is actually banned on some waters as it is deemed to be too effective! Fortunately, I have yet to hear of a strike indicator ban anywhere in South Africa, so we are free to use the technique – although I see few other anglers fishing this way.

Deep nymphing does, however, require patience. You will need to wait a while for the team of flies to sink, but keep a close eye on that indicator, as again, takes often occur on the drop. Retrieves need to be slow – the hand twist is ideal – with long pauses to allow the flies to keep a good depth. If you find yourself wanting to retrieve too quickly, try reciting the mantra adopted by American fly-fishing author, Dave Hughes: 'The slower the retrieve, the faster the fishing will be.' I promise you, it works!

This technique is suitable for fishing water between 6 and 14 feet. You can go a bit deeper by lengthening the section of tippet from the leader to the first fly. On occasion,

Rainbows are the more common dam stock. When I do get a brown, I can never resist taking a moment to admire the magnificent colours before gently releasing the fish. This one fell to deep nymphing tactics using a floating line, strike indicator and an 18-foot leader.

The water clarity in the Bottom Dam at Dondini is exceptional, so the fish can be quite skittish. Fortunately, a light breeze ruffled the surface on this day, but in flat, calm conditions it may be necessary to push out long casts to reach trout that are undisturbed by a kick boat.

I have used up to 22 feet in total leader/tippet length. Beyond that, even I agree that leader turnover becomes a pain – no matter how well you cast!

A couple more points on this method. Firstly, make sure you use a thin piece of yarn for the indicator; it *must* pass easily through the rod rings – otherwise you will find yourself having to handline the fish in the last few yards in order to net them! Also, you might well be wondering why you should go to all the trouble of fishing long leaders on a floating line, when you could easily use a fast-sinking line and get to the required depth more quickly. The answer lies in the *presentation*. With the long-leader/floating-line setup, as you retrieve the flies will move *upwards* – just as the hatching nymphs of many aquatic insect species will do. With a sinking line, your retrieve will pull the flies *horizontally* – a completely different type of presentation.

Anyway, as I said, this is slow, patient fishing – but absolutely deadly on its day … do give it a try.

SINKING LINE

Fishing a sinking line is the mainstay of stillwater fishing for most anglers. Various line sink rates are available. The slowest are the slightly negative-buoyancy intermediate lines, which sink at around 1 inch per second, through to high-density, ultra-fast sink lines that plummet to the depths at between 5 and 7 or more inches per second. Most popular are the medium and slow sink lines, but I don't use or even *own* one these days – and here's why.

For me, everything changed a decade or so ago with the introduction of that wonderful invention – the sinking braided leader, or Polyleader, used in conjunction with an intermediate line.

If you just want to fish subsurface, then use an intermediate Polyleader with the intermediate line. To prospect up to 8 feet deep, a slow-sink Polyleader works fine. If you want to fish water in the 8- to 20-foot range, then a super-fast sink Polyleader will rapidly drag the intermediate line down into the depths.

The advantage of having a set of Polyleaders handy is that it is very quick to change sinking rates. The Polyleaders are attached to the tip of the intermediate line by the usual loop-to-loop connection, so switching leaders only takes a moment. This is much easier than swapping reel spools between various lines to get the sink rate you want.

A Polyleader takes the intermediate line down *tip first*, so you can vary the retrieve speed, and therefore control

Rod position is important with sunk-line fishing. As the line sinks, hold the rod tip a few inches above the water to watch for visible takes on the line. Once you begin the retrieve, push the rod tip just under the surface to maintain direct contact, and detect takes by feel.

the depth at which the fly fishes right through the retrieve. With practice, you can even ease the fly up the edge of a channel or drop-off – a deadly method.

A standard medium sink line behaves very differently. After you have allowed the line to reach the required depth (say within a foot or two of the bottom) the *entire line* continues to sink, forming a belly below the depth of the fly. This means that if you retrieve slowly with a medium sink line, you will constantly catch up on weed or muck on the bottom, and foul the fly. The only way to avoid this is to pull back more quickly from about a third of the way through the retrieve. If Mr Trout wants a slow-moving fly on that day, then you are not going to have much success!

Before Polyleaders came on the scene, a similar presentation could be achieved by using a sink-tip line. Sink tips have 10 feet or more of fast-sinking line; the rest of the line is designed to float. They sound like a good idea – until you try to cast one; wild and uncontrollable would be a fair description. My sink tip wore out a dozen years ago, and I was very glad to see the last of it. I hear modern sink tips have improved somewhat in casting performance, but I still wouldn't consider swapping one for the versatile Polyleader.

I hope by now you are sold on Polyleaders and intermediate lines, so let's move on to tippet and fly presentations with this setup.

I generally fish unweighted or lightly weighted flies with sinking lines. You don't want to use a long tippet, otherwise the line will be down deep, but the fly will still be riding high in the water. I find about 5 feet is more or less right, and, once again, my choice is fluorocarbon in 2× or 3×.

As with the floating-line tactics, I often fish a second fly 6 feet behind the first, using the usual tying-on-at-the-bend-of-the-first-fly technique.

I also like to fish contrasting patterns and fly sizes with the tandem rig. These are some that have worked exceptionally well on a wide range of dams: size 8 Variegated Black Chenille Woolly Bugger teamed with a lightly weighted size 12 Vinyl Damsel on the point (usually my first choice on a dam I have not fished before). The same Woolly Bugger with a size 12 San Juan Worm can also work well. A Woolly Bugger/Zonker Dragon team is a good bet when you need lots of action to pull in fish from a distance. Lastly, if you are faced with very discoloured water from storm run-off or algae, then a Black Woolly Bugger/Yellow Zonker combination can be fantastic. I only got onto fishing yellow flies quite recently, after reading that they have been killing patterns at Grafham Water in England during algae blooms. Don't use yellow flies in clear water, though. You are likely to frighten more fish than you catch!

As I mentioned earlier, I skip the slow and medium sink lines these days, but I always carry a super fast sink Hi D line on a spare reel spool. Although I don't fish it often, the Hi D has two uses that can save the day when things are slow. Firstly, when trout want a fly presented fast and deep, it allows you to keep the fly well down throughout the retrieve. Use this technique with a natural grizzly Zonker or the Filoplume Fry when trout are minnow feeding. Also, at times during winter, male trout may become aggressive and whack an Orange Zonker or Orange Marabou Streamer retrieved fast and deep. Fishing this way, I don't bother with a tapered leader at all, and use 5 feet of heavy tippet – 1× or 2× fluorocarbon – attached directly to the Hi D line. Strong tippets are essential, as takes on a fast-retrieved streamer can be brutal.

The Hi D can also be used to fish the so-called 'booby style'. Booby flies have large twin 'eyes' made of buoyant plastazote, and a long marabou tail to give lots of action. I also use a floating dragon nymph made with a thick deer-hair body, which achieves a similar effect.

A very short tippet of about 2 feet is looped straight onto the Hi D. You cast out and let the line sink right to the bottom. The buoyant booby fly darts towards the bottom when you retrieve, and rises slowly in the water during pauses. I regard this as a minor tactic in my local KwaZulu-Natal waters, but booby-style fishing is practised more often, and apparently with greater success, in Mpumalanga. Deep-hooked fish are, unfortunately, rather common with this technique – another reason why I rarely use it.

Lastly, regarding sunk-line fishing in general: the position of the rod tip during the retrieve is important. After making the cast and waiting for the line to sink to the required depth, keep the rod tip about 3 inches above the surface. This will allow you to pick up takes on the drop. Often, you will not feel anything on the line, but you may see the line twitch or draw tight – requiring an instant strike. Once you begin the retrieve, push the rod tip just *under* the surface. This keeps direct contact with the line, and you will be able to detect even very gentle takes by feel.

DEADLY RETRIEVES

Finding the right retrieve for the day can make a huge difference to your catch. Get it right and you could get a load of fish. An inappropriate retrieve for the trout's current

I don't think they can be described as pretty, but buoyant flies such as the Booby Woolly Bugger (above) and Deer Hair Dragon (below) fished on a Hi D line, can save the day when things are slow.

mood might result in only a couple of takes, or nothing at all. The retrieve I see used most often is the fast 2-foot strip – many anglers seem to know little else. It does catch fish, but the problem I have with this retrieve is that there is no creature on the trout's menu that behaves in this way. Mayfly and damsel nymphs crawl or wriggle. Dragonfly nymphs use a form of jet propulsion that allows them to move rapidly, but only in jerky bursts of a few inches. Any minnow being chased by a trout simply belts away into the nearest cover without stopping. There is nothing that goes *zip*, stop, *zip*, stop, in 2-foot movements. This method of fishing is boring for the angler, and I have a strong feeling that it may be just as boring for the fish as well!

Few anglers would want to go fishing with just one fly pattern in their fly box. In the same way, a good repertoire of *imitative* retrieve techniques will add variety and interest to your fishing, and undoubtedly improve catches. The following are the ones that work best for me.

Hand twist

Probably the most versatile and effective stillwater retrieve worldwide. I estimate that 80% of my stillwater trout are taken on the hand twist. You start by gripping the line between thumb and forefinger, and twist your wrist to catch the line against your little finger, at the same time drawing down to pull on the line. You will find that this action results in a little loop of line in your hand, which you need to drop before repeating the process.

If this sounds complicated, study the sequence of pictures above, and practise until you are able to move the line continuously. It is one of those things that is like riding a bicycle – once mastered, you'll never forget it. The beauty of the technique is that you can move the line smoothly at a snail's pace – great when fishing small nymphs. By speeding up the action, the retrieve becomes jerkier, but still gives a continuous movement. This imparts an irresistible pulsing action to Woolly Buggers, Dragon Nymphs and Zonker patterns.

Strip retrieves

Strip retrieves are the easiest to learn, as you are simply moving the fly by pulling on the line. However, you should not be restricted to the 2-foot strip retrieve.

I have done well with two or three slow twitches of a couple of inches, followed by a long pause. Also *twitch, twitch,* and then a slow pull of about a foot of line can be good.

If this fails to get a response, a long, slow pull may work.

Take your retrieving hand far away from your body as you steadily draw in about 5 feet of line in a smooth, continuous movement. When fishing attractor or minnow imitations, the same long pull, but this time executed with a little more speed, can also work nicely.

Yet another variation is to repeatedly give the line short pulls – as fast as you can. This gives a strong pulsing action with Marabou and Zonker patterns.

Strip and hang

This retrieve is the wild card. I have known it to out-fish all other methods on some days, and at other times it doesn't seem to work at all. Pioneered by veteran UK competition angler, Bob Church, the strip-and-hang technique is most effective when fishing a sinking line over deep water from a kick boat or other watercraft. The technique works as follows.

Cast out a fair distance, and let the line sink to within a foot of the bottom. Begin with a normal slow retrieve, hand twist, or whatever you fancy. When you judge your fly to be about 8 yards from the rod tip, strip the line three or four times *as fast as you can*. On the last strip, lift the rod high to give extra

acceleration – and then *stop and hold* (this is the 'hang' part). The theory behind this retrieve is that trout often follow a rapidly moving fly without taking it. As the fly accelerates, the fish keeps pace right behind. When you stop abruptly, the fast-moving fish has two choices – either grab the fly or go sailing past, as it can't stop as abruptly as your fly just has. The take usually comes within a second of stopping. It pays to leave the fly 'on the hang' for about 15 seconds, as sometimes a trout will circle a few times before making up its mind. Takes vary from a gentle lifting of the line to fish hitting so hard that the rod tip is pulled right into the water. Try not to strike back hard at these aggressive takes, as the likely outcome is a smashed tippet!

Ripping it back

Also known as 'hand over hand', 'milking the cow', or 'Cornish knitting' (who thinks up these names?), this high-speed retrieve technique is well known to saltwater fly-fishers. At first, 'ripping it back' was considered by some to be unethical when applied to trout, but of late, the method has gained acceptance. To counter the purists I would argue that this is, in fact, an *imitative* retrieve when fishing minnow imitations.

Place the rod under your casting arm, and simply haul in line hand over hand. The faster you can do this the better the retrieve seems to work. The only problem is striking, as you are not actually holding the rod. Takes are felt very positively by a tug on the line, and while you can make an attempt at striking by twisting your body to one side (but this would be impossible in a float tube!), I generally just tug back without any attempt at moving the rod. This gives me a good ratio of hook-ups.

Ripping it back works very well when trout are actively chasing minnows – the Filoplume Fry is deadly with this method. Also – for reasons that I can't begin to fathom – it often works when water temperatures are high. So well, in fact, that I have known this retrieve to catch the only fish of the day when trout are apparently lethargic from warm water.

Slow continuous retrieve

How many times have you fished away for a couple of hours without so much as a tweak on the line, decided to reel in – and immediately got a take? On some days, our fussy friends want only a fly with continuous movement, and when they do, try the following.

Reach forward with the rod. Trap the line with your index finger (on the hand holding the rod), and draw the rod towards you. *At the same time*, reach forward with your other hand, and as soon as the rod butt is level with your body, begin retrieving line. While you are pulling on the line, push the rod forward to begin the cycle again. Like the hand twist, this is a difficult retrieve to describe – the photo sequence above should make things clearer. By alternately pulling in line with the rod, and then with your hand, it is possible to achieve a very steady continuous line retrieve.

BANK FISHING

A common mistake when stillwater fishing from a bank is to assume that the fish will always be a long way out. Many anglers start by wading out as far as possible and then making the longest cast they can manage.

In fact, if the fish are working the bank margin, the chances are that the trout *were* patrolling in 2 or 3 feet of water – right where you are now standing! They will by now, of course, be gone. Remember that the most productive food areas are the shallows, so undisturbed trout often actively feed very close in. Therefore, it is usually best to fish through the very shallow water first without wading. Keep low to avoid spooking fish, and be on the lookout for boils, swirls or rises of active fish.

If the water is clear, there is a good chance of spotting cruising trout. For this, polarised sunglasses are essential. Dark grey lenses are best when it is sunny. In overcast conditions, pale amber polarised glasses are fantastic – they enhance contrast and cut through the silvery glare reflected back from an overcast sky. Many anglers report getting headaches when using amber lenses on a sunny day, so you really do need to carry both types.

Linda Hill is very wisely using a line-stripping tray to fish from a rocky dam wall. This avoids almost certain tangles that would result as line is retrieved – and also enhances casting distance.

... and the result – a respectable 4-pound rainbow on her third cast of the day. It is important to unhook and release a fish in the water – lifting a trout onto a rocky bank could cause great damage.

When you do spot a fish, it is important to 'lead' by casting ahead of it. Never cast *at* the fish – trout in the shallows are vulnerable to predators, and are easily spooked. If a trout is casually sipping flies from the surface, a suitable dry-fly cast about 10 feet ahead of its path should work fine. For deep-cruising fish, a weighted nymph is a better bet – you might need to lead the fish by as much as 50 feet to allow the nymph to sink to the trout's cruising depth.

If you are not getting action in the shallows, then by all means start firing casts out into deeper water and wade a bit if possible. Wading a dam needs to be done with some care; a firm, gravelly margin in the shallows can suddenly turn to soft, oozing mud when you get in waist deep. I know it makes you look like an old codger, but a wading staff or walking stick is a pretty sensible idea for deep wading. Better to test the ground first before stepping into armpit-deep, gooey mud!

Like all stillwater fishing, location is essential to success. If you don't see any signs of activity, or you are not catching fish, don't stay in one place and flog away. *Move*, and keep on moving until you find the action.

Floating and intermediate lines are best for bank fishing. Only on very rare occasions, such as dredging the deep water from a dam wall, will I go to a fast-sinking line from the bank. Talking of lines, a constant bank-fishing problem is what to do with all that loose line as you strip back on the retrieve. If you are standing on the bank, you can be guaranteed that it will get caught up on grasses, twigs or rocks. When wading, any sinking line – even an intermediate – will, of course, sink to the bottom. If you are like me, you will probably end up stepping on it as well. None of this is good when you plan to shoot out all that slack on the next cast.

A line-stripping tray that straps to your waist is a useful accessory. They do look a bit ridiculous, but then many of us already look that way just by donning neoprene waders. With the exception of the garb worn by ardent cyclists, body-hugging neoprenes must be the most unflattering sportswear imaginable. I stopped drinking beer three years ago – so how come when I slip into my neoprene waders I suddenly develop very visible middle-aged spread? Some things in life are just not fair!

FLOAT-TUBE AND KICK-BOAT FISHING

If someone told you that you could treble your stillwater catches *and* be able to stealthily fish anywhere on a dam, regardless of wind direction, *and* never ever get caught up on trees, bushes or tall grass on your back cast, you would, of course, jump at the opportunity. That is what float tubes and kick boats can do for you. In a word, they are brilliant!

In this section I would like to take a look at a couple of the more advanced techniques available to tubers and kick boaters, but first a few pointers for folks who are new to the game. For a start, don't overinflate your tube. Be especially aware of changes in air pressure with altitude and temperature. For example, if you live in Durban, and fully inflate your tube at home before driving to an Underberg trout venue, you will have climbed 1 600 metres or more, and may well have popped or at least badly stressed your float tube by the time you reach your destination. By the same token, leaving a tube in the sun on dry land while you take a lunch break has also resulted in many a popped tube. Leave the tube in the water during breaks, and let a bit of air out as the temperature rises during the day.

A smallish, weed-free dam and a calm day are essential for a maiden voyage, as is a firm, gently shelving bank from which to launch. Gently fin your way out. You will, of course, be travelling backwards, but don't worry – you'll soon get used to it. Fin with steady strokes and avoid splashing the water. Try not to overdo it on the first few outings; finning seems to use leg muscles that you didn't know you had, even if you are relatively fit from regularly walking. If at any time you feel uneasy (a few folk do get a bit panicky in a tube) or tired, then come straight in and take a break. Don't tube alone – at least, not until you have become very experienced, and *always* wear a lifejacket or buoyancy aid.

You might find the low position a little awkward for casting at first, but you will very soon get used to that as well. Practise casting without rocking your body. Rocking a tube when casting causes waves to spread across a calm dam – and that does not impress the trout at all.

There are just a few problems to watch out for, namely, thunder storms, weed and wind. With an approaching storm, the answer is simple – get out fast! Some years ago there was a very stupid story going around that you are safe in a thunder storm in a tube (perhaps because the original doughnut float tubes were made out of rubber truck tyres?). Utter nonsense. *Any* fishing in a storm with a graphite rod

is extremely dangerous. Sitting in the middle of a dam with a potential lightning conductor in your hand is lunacy – get out of there!

Weed is not dangerous, but it can be an absolute pain. Because you travel backwards, it is pretty easy to fin your way straight into a thick weedbed. Your fins will get stuck in the stuff. Don't panic. Try to gently turn around and push your way back out with the fins. Experienced tubers learn to look over their shoulder from time to time to avoid this hassle!

Kick boats and tubes have a low centre of gravity, and are stable in wind and waves – possibly more so than many small boats – so again, wind does not present any great danger, except perhaps on a huge dam during a gale. If the wind really gets up, you might find it impossible to fin your way back, though, in which case, go with the wind. When you reach the shore, carry your tube back along the bank. It is for this reason that I fish small dams from my fin-powered U tube. I always tackle large water with my sneaker motor-powered kick boat. I still wear fins with the kick boat, of course, but this is mainly to make adjustments to drift and fishing positions. If the weather turns bad, I can put the motor on high speed, relax and enjoy the ride back to the launching spot.

Experienced anglers know precisely how hard they can play a trout without breaking the tippet or having the hook pull out. This powerful 6-pound rainbow gave Roger Baert quite a tussle, but he soon had the fish safely in the net.

A big storm can blow in quickly in the high country. Lightning is a very real danger when you are waving a graphite rod around in the middle of a dam, and this looming sky is a warning to get off the water. Don't take chances out there.

For those already well versed in this branch of the sport, I would like to ask you a question. How do you go about fishing from a tube or kick boat? The most common technique I see is where the angler steadily fins along and makes fairly short casts right into the water he or she has just finned through. This does catch some trout, but I think it is a mistake to imagine that you are invisible to the fish just because you're in a tube. Tubes and kick boats *do* scare trout – they just bother them a bit less than conventional boats.

Let me introduce you to a concept – I'm going to call it the Circle of Scared Trout (CST). The chances are that the CST is high within a 5-yard radius of your tube. Most of the fish very close to you will be aware of your presence, and have probably decided to make themselves scarce. If you move out to between 5 and 10 yards, the CST proportion will be lower – only a few fish may have spotted you. At 15 yards plus, the CST factor is usually about nil, because you are probably beyond the trout's range of vision. Therefore, I prefer to push out longer casts than most float tubers – about 18 yards or so. I find this a comfortable cast without straining for distance. I catch the great majority of fish on the part of the retrieve from 18 yards to 10. As my flies get closer to the tube, the chances of a take diminish significantly.

When fishing exceptionally clear water on a flat, calm day, I have seen trout spook from my kick boat at 15 yards (always wearing polarised glasses can tell you a lot about what is going on!). Thankfully, this is rather rare, but if I notice it happening, I put some beef into my casting and aim for 20 yards plus. The CST diminishes greatly in dirty and wind-ruffled water – so you may well pick up plenty of trout within 10 yards in these more forgiving conditions.

Continuing with tactics, I prefer to fish undisturbed water. This means having a strategy for your fishing. Plan a drift path and turn so that you have your back to the wind. Fire out a fairly long cast (casting with a tail wind makes this easy), and hold position by steadily finning. Allow the flies to sink to the required depth and retrieve. Then let the wind push you along a few yards and repeat the sequence. Once you get into a fish it pays to hold that position for a while and make several casts into the same area – you might have hit a hot spot.

When fish are active in the bank-side shallows and weed margins, I set up a drift about 15 yards from the shore and cast across the kick boat back into the shallows. I let the wind push me along so that I am constantly covering new water. The nice thing about these craft is that it is so easy to adjust a drift path; all it takes is a gentle push of the fins, and after a while, you will learn to do it almost unconsciously.

A useful technique when the trout are very deep is to cast, let the flies sink way down, and retrieve only a couple of yards of line. Give a couple of kicks with your fins and feed out the slack line. Then retrieve a couple of yards again, kick and feed out the slack, and simply keep repeating the process. This method works very well with the floating-line deep-nymph method as well as fishing with an intermediate line and fast-sinking Polyleader. With the latter, I find I can keep the flies working at 20 feet or more. It just takes a little patience to give the line time to sink to that depth. Fishing this way will mean that you *are* fishing water that you have just paddled through, but when the trout are very deep they seem far less easily spooked.

I don't think this technique can be regarded as trolling (using the movement of a boat to trail flies without casting); you are making the retrieve manually, and merely using the tube or kick boat to take up slack during pauses. Trolling is regarded by some as 'unsporting' and banned on many waters. In fact I have seen fishery regulations where all the rules are in normal type except for 'NO TROLLING!', which is printed in capitals – so this is something to watch out for.

BOAT FISHING

Back in England, I used to do quite a lot of boat fishing on the big reservoirs. Since moving to South Africa in the mid-1980s, I doubt I have trout fished from a boat more than a dozen times. Most South African trout dams are smaller than 50 hectares and are, I believe, more effectively fished from a float tube or kick boat.

There are, however, a couple of situations where I would choose to use a boat rather than a float tube. The trouble with boats, however, is that they are noisy – and I'm not talking about outboard motors here. Rather, any movement *in* the boat, such as a heavy footfall, dropping a landing net, or even just rowing, is telegraphed through the water, and frightens the fish. Also, boats drift uncontrollably in wind, so you are often forced to anchor, or constantly use the oars to adjust the drift – a noisy and very tiresome process if you want to regularly move fishing spots.

Having said that, I prefer a boat on dams with extensive weed margins growing right to the surface. This is a big problem for tubers and kick boaters. Your fins get caught up in the weed, and it can be a horrible battle to make any headway. A rowing boat will glide over the surface weed,

allowing you to reach open water easily. The other situation in which I am not comfortable using a kick boat is on a truly huge dam. And while there are few 100-hectare-plus trout waters in this country, when I do fish such places I feel more at ease in a boat with a small petrol-driven outboard motor – preferably with an additional electric sneaker motor to get into fishing position. What we are looking at here is essentially a fully kitted bass boat. Quite a number of our trout dams do offer the use of a boat for those without their own floatation devices. Unfortunately, these may be ill equipped. There will be a set of oars (well, I would hope so!), but often no anchor. I have used a makeshift anchor from a brick attached to a length of cheap cord from a hardware store. This holds well if you anchor over weed. Also, should you choose to fish on the drift, you will find that the boat spins uncontrollably in wind – really irritating if two anglers are trying to fish from one boat. A plastic bucket attached to cord let out from the bow is an effective improvisation for drogue fishing techniques, which have been fine-tuned to an art in England ('proper' drogues are mini underwater 'parachutes' made from rectangular cloth, that slow and control drift). The drag from the bucket will ensure a straight drift at a manageable speed.

FIGHTING FISH

In the old days, we used to hear anglers boasting, 'Yeah, I caught an 8-pound brown trout and it took me *40 minutes* to land it'. This would have been considered an epic and memorable battle with a big fish. Today, with the increasing

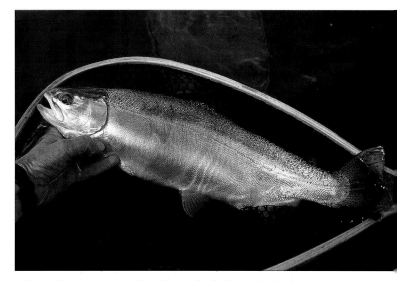

A fin-perfect 5-pound rainbow from a fertile high-altitude dam. Stocked as a fingerling only two years previously, this fish could grow to double this weight in a couple of years.

It is easy to fish from a boat in flat, calm conditions, although you will need to make a careful, stealthy approach to avoid spooking the trout. When the wind gets up, it is necessary to anchor or use a drogue to prevent an excessively fast and uncontrollable drift.

trend to release trout, such a tale could be greeted with a frown. After 40 minutes, that fish would have been utterly exhausted, and the chance of a successful release about zero. To release trout, you need to get 'em in as fast as possible. This means playing trout *hard* – but stopping *just* short of the point where you are likely to break the tippet, or have the hook open up or pull out.

Nine times out of 10, the first thing that happens when you hook into a nice trout is that the fish will want to run. Let it – but apply steady pressure by feathering the line as it slips through your retrieving hand. With luck, the trout will run away from you, taking up the slack line created while retrieving. You will now have the fish 'on the reel' – a much safer situation than having a lot of slack line lying at your feet or on a stripping tray. Loose line can easily get tangled during the fight.

As I mentioned in the Gearing Up chapter (*see* page 8), I never play a trout using the drag on the reel. Adjust the drag setting to 'light'; it needs to give just enough resistance to stop a possible over-run. You can exert very precise line tension by palming the spool rim – or applying pressure to the rim with your index finger. Remember to keep your hand

clear of the rapidly spinning reel handle, or you will get a good rap on the knuckles! If the trout is a particularly feisty one, you might find all the fly line is off the reel and you are well into the backing. When things get to this stage, you will need to ease off a bit on the finger pressure on the reel. Remember the backing will be peeling off a smaller diameter of the reel spindle, so braking the reel will greatly increase tension on the line.

Very occasionally – and probably just to keep us on our toes – a trout's first move will be to run straight at the angler, in which case, forget all about trying to get that fish on the reel, and strip in line – *fast*! Don't let the line go slack for even a moment – with barbless or micro-barbed hooks, the fish is very likely to 'fall off'. There is a school of thought that says, 'always play fish on the reel', but if you have lots of line lying around from the retrieve, I think it is better to keep tight to the fish by stripping line.

Once the first run stops, *then* start piling on the pressure, either by winding like crazy on the reel or by stripping line – whatever seems appropriate to the situation. Keep the rod up, and be alert for more sudden runs. The key to landing fish quickly is to let a trout run against steady, controlled pressure when it wants to, and at all other times, *you* take charge by really bending the rod into that trout. You might break off on a few at first before you find out just how much you can pressure a fish. Once you get the hang of fighting a fish really hard, you should find you lose a lot less through hooks falling out or trout diving into snags or weed. I have noticed that the anglers who are scared to put more than just a slight bend into the rod are the ones who are most likely to lose fish – as well as kill them by prolonging the fight.

While on the topic, there are a couple more points I'd like to make. Browns in stillwater generally don't give you too many problems; with them, you can expect a head-shaking fight, and sometimes a bit of thrashing around on the surface. However, the medium-sized rainbows often jump repeatedly while ripping line from the reel. If you get a jumper, lower the rod a fraction to reduce line tension. This should prevent a possible break-off if the fish comes crashing down on the tippet.

A different problem is less easily solved. On some very weedy dams, fish may dive straight into weed as soon as you hook them. It can be a case of 'Fish on!' and, within a second or so, 'Oh no, it's weeded, and it's come off!' In a real-life situation, this phrase would be followed by a few well-chosen expletives! What may help is to plunge the rod tip down into the water, so that you are pulling *down* on the fish, rather than up, as you would with the rod held in the usual high position. Often, the trout will respond by coming straight to the surface and jumping. I can't promise success every time, but I have got some big fish out of very heavy weed using this technique. You need to act fast, though. As soon as you get a hook-up, plunge that rod tip down as deep as you can – don't even wait a second or the trout may have already made up its mind to dive into the weeds.

SPECIALISED TECHNIQUES FOR WINTER TROUT

The winter season creates exciting opportunities to stalk visible trout. Dams that carry a fair amount of colour from summer storm run-off and algae may become crystal clear from June through to August. Added to this, trout often group over the gravel and shale margins while they go through the motions of spawning. In many of our still waters, winter is the only time that you can sight-fish effectively.

Before we look at tactics, I would like to consider an ethical issue regarding fishing for winter spawners. Is it right to attempt to catch these fish? Since trout very rarely spawn successfully in dams, I believe it is acceptable. After all, it is not going to affect the future breeding stock of the fishery,

A hook-up, and I am making no attempt to stop the first run. I need to be careful as I am fishing a 5× tippet with a tiny nymph! Steady pressure is applied by braking the reel rim with my index finger.

A couple more short runs against increasing pressure from braking the reel, and the fish's head is up, and I quickly slide it into the net. Even on such light tackle the total playing time is under 3 minutes.

The tiny hook is gently slipped out with the fish still under water in the net. A quick pose for a snap – and the fat rainbow swims off making a splash that has me wiping water from my sunglasses!

as stillwaters rely on artificial stocking. Rivers, however, are a different story. Most rivers are closed during the winter season, but where fishing *is* allowed, I believe that fish on the spawning redds should be left well alone. Disturbing spawning river trout could have a catastrophic effect on wild, self-sustaining fisheries.

The standard tactic for catching stillwater trout sighted over gravel is to use an **egg pattern**, particularly the well-known Egg Fly (also called a Glow Bug, after the yarn used to tie them). Trout actively mop up eggs shed by rival gravid hen trout. Such behaviour seems repulsive in human terms, but is very common in the animal kingdom. It is all about propagating your own genes by eliminating the opposition. Anglers can capitalise on the trout's instinctive urge by presenting what is, essentially, a tiny orange ball of fluff. On most occasions, this is sufficient to fool trout into thinking they are consuming a rival's egg.

The key to presenting egg patterns is that they are taken most readily 'on the drop' as they sink, or suspended under a strike indicator at the trout's cruising depth. Any sideways movement by retrieving – even wind drift on the line – usually results in a rejection, or it completely spooks the trout.

Reaction to egg patterns can be unpredictable. If a fish has never seen this fly before, it may zoom over and swallow it without hesitation. Just a few weeks ago (I'm writing this

in winter), I went to a private dam where I spotted three trout circling over gravel at the dam outlet. They were so naïve that they actually sat on the bottom and *chewed* on the Egg Fly – probably wondering why it tasted of nothing – giving only the slightest quiver on my strike indicator. Clearly they had never encountered anything like this before. I soon caught and released all three fish. The best was just a shade under 5 pounds, and the smallest 3 1/2 pounds – not bad for less than half an hour's fishing.

On hard-fished waters, the reaction may be very different. An 'educated' trout will inhale and spit out an Egg Fly in a fraction of a second, as soon as it learns it is not the real thing. This requires a lightning strike, and it is common to miss many takes. Educated trout may even ignore an egg pattern completely, or flee at the mere sight of the fly. It is often thought that trout preoccupied by spawning will not feed on insects or any other usual food item. When egg patterns fail, I have had surprisingly good success with tiny imitative nymphs – size 16 Flash-back Hare's Ears and Superglue Midge Pupa in particular. It seems spawning trout *can* be enticed to feed, but become very wary of large, conventional flies when they are on the gravel beds.

Not every trout in the dam is likely to be cruising the gravel patches in winter. Also, of course, many dams lack these features entirely, so at times you may have to blind-search the water. The common wisdom is to fish orange streamers in winter to induce an aggressive territorial reaction from the fish. The Whisky Fly is a favourite old standard. I prefer an Orange Zonker, or a UK pattern called the Vindaloo. The latter is so simple to tie that I thought it unnecessary to include it as a fly recipe feature. The Vindaloo has a wing and tail of the hottest fluorescent orange marabou you can find. The body is orange chenille – again the brightest, most garish stuff you can lay your hands on. If you want to get fancy about it, you can add a few strands of Krystal Flash to the wing as well. My experience with orange streamers is that they are effective on less than 20% of the dams I fish. When they do work, they can out-fish any other winter fly. The rest of the time, they just seem to frighten the trout – and, looking at a horrid creation like the Vindaloo, I can understand why! Generally, I do better searching for winter trout with the usual old perennial winners like Black Woolly Buggers, Damsel Nymphs and Hare's Ears.

Fighting a fish taken on a size 14 Egg Fly. The trout were patrolling a gravel patch about a yard from the bank. I stood well back from the water and made a cast along the bank.

WHAT TO DO WHEN NOTHING WORKS

We all get the odd blank day. At times, there may not be much you can do about it. The water temperature might be

Sight-fishing the shallows. Notice I am crouching to keep out of the trout's vision (left). Can you spot the swirl of an approaching fish to the right of the wooden posts? A size 14 Superglue Midge Pupa fished static under a tiny strike indicator soon picks up a small rainbow (centre and right) – good fun on a 2-weight outfit.

too high (in which case you probably should not be fishing a dam anyway) or a severe algae bloom could have depleted oxygen levels, making the trout lethargic. Occasionally, the trout may just 'switch off' during a flat calm.

However, there are times when trout are active, but simply refuse any fly presented in the conventional manner. I am thinking particularly of small, clear dams that have been subjected to very heavy fishing pressure. Many of the dam's trout population could have been caught and released a dozen times, and will have learnt – the hard way – to be cautious. Usually, the first flies to stop working are the large streamers that everyone uses – size 8 Mrs Simpsons, Walkers, Killers and, I hate to say it because it is one of my favourite patterns, the Woolly Bugger.

The next stage usually sees success with slowly retrieved small imitative patterns. You might catch on size 12 Damsel Nymphs, size 14 or 16 Hare's Ears and so on. Eventually, the trout get wise to these tactics as well, and you begin to hear anglers moaning that the fish have become 'uncatchable'.

The difficulty seems to be that, no matter what retrieve or fly is used, it is impossible to exactly imitate the wriggle of a real midge larva, or the swimming action of a live damsel nymph – to give a couple of examples. The solution to the problem is a simple one: you do not retrieve at all. Fish a nymph suspended under a strike indicator at the trout's cruising depth and just cast it out and leave it. At times I have done well with this technique using small San Juan Worms and Hare's Ears, but the most effective fly group by far appears to be the midge pupa imitations. The Superglue Midge has been the best I have discovered to date. I used the Epoxy Midge (an earlier incarnation of the same fly) for many years, but the new Superglue version appears to have a definite edge. There are a couple of problems with this technique. The first is that it takes

enormous concentration and some patience, because you are not actually *doing* anything. We fly-fishers are used to being busy all day, casting and retrieving, casting and retrieving … To just chuck out a fly and leave it suspended is not something we easily adapt to. However, takes can come right out of the blue using this technique, and when they do, they are often very quick. You will need to concentrate hard on the strike indicator and react fast before the trout ejects the fly. This is where the second problem arises.

When striking fast, most of us tend to strike too hard, and break off on a lot of fish. The answer is the **slip-strike** technique. Instead of holding the line in the usual way in the rod hand – which tends to 'lock' the line as you squeeze the rod handle to strike – you just catch the line between your first two fingers. Exactly the same as if you were holding a cigarette (if, like me, you are still a smoker, you will find you can do this instinctively!).

What we have here is a built-in 'slipping clutch'. It is impossible to hold the line tightly enough to cause a break off. By the way, this is also a great technique for avoiding smashing your tippet when fishing static dry flies as well as the Egg Fly tactics covered earlier.

So here we have a specialised method for catching very educated trout. I would not care to use a static Midge Pupa all the time, as it is hardly the most exciting way to fish. However, it certainly beats having a blank day. After paging back through my fishing log it is interesting to note some catches made using this method: 11 rainbows – including fish of 7 pounds 12 ounces, and 6 pounds – in a morning's fishing, and so on. Like any angler, I am giving you one of my *best ever* catches using these tactics. I'm not mentioning all the days when I only got a couple of 2-pounders on the static pupa … but then, even a couple of 2-pounders beats a total blank, right?

PARACHUTE HOPPER
Originator: Ed Schroeder, USA.
Hook: 8, **10**, **12** Tiemco 3761 or similar 2× long heavy wire nymph hook.
Thread: 6/0 brown.
Wing post: White calf body hair (standard dressing), or orange Poly yarn.
Body: Pale hare's fur.
Rib: Yellow vinyl tube.
Wing: Pale mottled turkey feather section, treated with Dave's Flexament.
Legs: Ginger cock saddle hackle, trimmed short and knotted to form 'knee'.
Hackle: Grizzly cock, wound parachute style.
Tying tip: This is a complex and difficult pattern to tie. If you have trouble getting the legs to lie in the correct position, try Superglue! I would expect each fly to take between 15 and 20 minutes to complete – but I promise you it's worth all the trouble!
Commercially tied alternatives: I have not seen the Parachute Hopper on sale in this country. You should be able to buy deer-hair hoppers, such as the Dave's Hopper.
When and how to fish this pattern: Most effective fished static dry, but also try giving it the occasional twitch. Best from early summer to late autumn. Takes are often explosive – use the 'slip strike' technique to avoid smashed tippets.

YELLOW ZONKER
Originator: Dan Byford, USA.
Hook: 8, 10 Tiemco 3761 or similar 2× long heavy wire nymph hook.
Thread: 6/0 black.
Body: Gold Mylar tubing, coated with 5-minute epoxy.
Wing: Yellow rabbit Zonker strip, secured at head and tail.
Hackle: Grizzly.
Head: Gold bead (optional), stick-on eyes (optional).
Tying tips: Although this is a fairly straightforward pattern, it takes a little practice to get the correct tension and alignment on the Zonker strip. Other colour combinations I often use are: Orange Zonker: Pearl Mylar body, orange Zonker strip, and red hackle. Olive Zonker: Green Fritz body, Olive Zonker strip, olive partridge hackle, and the Standard Zonker: Pearl Mylar tube body, natural (grizzly) Zonker strip, and grizzly hackle.
Commercially tied alternatives: Commercially tied Zonkers are on sale at most fly shops.
When and how to fish this pattern: The Yellow Zonker is an outstanding fly in very discoloured water. Don't use it in clear water on skittish trout – it will probably frighten the life out of them! The orange version can be deadly in winter. The standard pattern is effective at any time of the year when trout are fry feeding. Best retrieves for Zonkers are the long slow strip, quick jerky strip or hand twist. Also, try the ripping it back retrieve – as fast as you can!

SUPERGLUE MIDGE PUPA
Originator: Superglue Midge Pupae are very popular and deadly generic UK patterns. The tying shown here is the one I have found most effective for local waters.
Hook: Size 12, **14**, **16** Kamazan B110 or similar heavy wire curved caddis hook.
Thread: 6/0 or 8/0 red.
Abdomen: Stripped peacock herl from eye of sword feather wound from bend of hook.
Thorax: Several turns of red Flexifloss (Spanflex) to create bulging thorax.
Wing case: Stripe across top of abdomen with black permanent marker pen.
Breather filaments: Small tuft of white marabou protruding from eye.
Tying tips: Coat body with thin layer of Superglue. When dry, apply thin coat of clear nail varnish. Be careful to avoid breather filaments as these need to remain mobile. By substituting the white marabou with a longer plume of natural CDC, the same tying makes an excellent subsurface midge emerger.
Commercially tied alternatives: Probably none, unless you want to import flies from the UK! Dubbed fur and silk body midge pupa imitations are on sale here, but I have found them to be far less effective than the Superglue Midge.
When and how to fish this pattern: A deadly pattern when there is midge activity. Fish static or with very slow hand twist under a strike indicator. Especially effective when dams become crystal clear in the winter months.

FILOPLUME FRY
Originator: Basil Hancock, SA.
Hook: Size 8, **10**, 12 Tiemco 3761 or similar 2× long heavy wire nymph hook.
Thread: 6/0 white.
Tail: Natural (undyed) grizzly marabou (also known as Chickaboo), plus 4 strands of pearl Krystal Flash.
Underbody: Tying thread.
Body: Grizzly marabou filoplume (secondary feather). The feathers are fragile and rather short, so you may need to tie in up to three in a row to complete the body.
Rib: Silver French tinsel.
Head: Small to medium gold bead.
Tying tips: Wind the rib very tight and in opposite direction to the delicate filoplume, otherwise after one trout the whole fly will come undone!
Commercially tied alternatives: None, but many other fry imitations are available, including the well-known Zonker, and Robin Fick's White Death – a very simple fly consisting of a white chenille body and a wing of white marabou and pearl Krystal Flash.
When and how to fish this pattern: Don't be put off by the 'bottle brush' appearance of the Filoplume Fry – when in the water the mobile feathers positively pulse with irresistible action. This pattern out-fishes any other fry imitation that I have tried! Use any time when you suspect trout are minnow feeding – often this peaks in autumn and early winter. Fish with intermediate or fast-sinking line. Effective retrieves are fast hand twist, long strip and ripping it back.

SAN JUAN WORM
Originator: Chuck Rizuto, USA.
Hook: Size 10, **12**, 14 Kamazan B110 or similar heavy wire curved caddis hook.
Thread: 6/0 red wound along length of body, and then ribbed tightly over chenille.
Body: Red Tuff chenille.
Weight: None.
Tying tips: For durability, apply clear nail varnish to the underside of the hook when you have completed the fly. Seal ends of chenille by singeing with a cigarette lighter. The standard tying incorporates a 'tail' of chenille at the eye of the hook as well. I find after one trout – or even just some energetic casting – this tends to bend upwards and cause the fly to spin unnaturally. I prefer to trim the chenille close to the hook eye.
Commercially tied alternatives: This pattern is commercially available.
When and how to fish this pattern: A tried-and-trusted midge larva imitation. Fish close to the bottom with a slow hand twist on a floating or intermediate line. Effective right through the year. On some dams, the San Juan Worm out-fishes all other patterns; on other waters it seems not to work at all. During winter, try a lime-green Tuff chenille variant, as tiny bright green midge larvae are abundant during the colder months.

ZONKER DRAGON NYMPH
Originator: Charles Jardine, UK. **Variant:** Nigel Dennis. SA.
Hook: Size **8** short shank, heavy wire.
Thread: 6/0 dark olive.
Tail: Olive grizzly rabbit Zonker strip.
Thorax and head: Dubbed mix of 70% olive rabbit fur, 30% olive SLF.
Abdomen: Olive Fritz chenille.
Hackle: Olive-dyed partridge.
Wing case: Olive Antron yarn.
Eyes: Heavy black-burnt mono, or medium black bead eyes on mono stalk. Alternatively, lead dumbbell eyes – to give a lively deep-diving action.
Weight: None.
Tying tip: This is an easy, straightforward pattern to tie. The original Charles Jardine pattern was a damsel imitation. My tying is similar but chunkier and intended to imitate the big dragon nymphs so common in South African waters.
Commercially tied alternatives: None, however, there are many generic Dragon Nymphs available. The Filoplume Dragon is an excellent commercially tied pattern.
When and how to fish this pattern: A good pattern when you need high visibility to draw trout in from a distance. Works year round fished near the bottom. Best retrieves are a jerky hand twist, twitch and pause and slow strip.

EGG FLY

Originator: First tied as a pattern to imitate salmon eggs that are heavily predated by rainbows in Alaskan rivers during the spawning run.
Hook: Size 12, **14**, **16** Kamazan B110 or similar heavy wire curved caddis hook.
Thread: 6/0 red.
Body: Steelhead Orange Glow Bug Yarn, chopped and dubbed, then clipped to form a round ball.
Weight: 2 to 4 turns lead wire, depending on fly size.
Tying tip: For such a simple pattern, the Egg Fly can be surprisingly tricky to tie well. The aim is to produce a perfect sphere. An alternative tying method is to place a section of yarn over the hook and flare it by tightly wrapping the tying silk. I find the dubbed version more durable. The Egg Fly is commercially tied, but often the fly-shop versions are too large to effectively imitate a trout egg.
When and how to fish this pattern: A specialised fly for winter spawners. Fish 'on the drop' to sighted fish or suspended under a strike indicator.

CDC MIDGE

Originator: Rene Harrop, USA.
Hook: 14, **16**, **18**, **20** Tiemco 100 or other fine wire dry fly.
Thread: 8/0 black.
Body: Stripped peacock herl.
Wing: Dun CDC.
Hackle: Two turns black cock, trimmed underneath fly.
Thorax: Black Superfine dubbing.
Tying tip: Tying tiny flies can be difficult and fiddling. When tying a batch of CDC Midges I usually start with the more manageable 16s, and then work my way down to size 20. Grey and cream midges are common on many waters. I imitate these by using an appropriate dubbing colour for the thorax, and substituting the back hackle for a grizzly.
Commercially tied alternatives: Small midge imitations are not easy to find in the shops. You should be able to purchase the Griffiths Gnat – a fly that in fact imitates a cluster of midges, but is nonetheless very effective.
When and how to fish this pattern: Use any time when small midges are hatching. Fish static dry to rising fish on a light tippet.

HOLOGRAPHIC HARE'S EAR

Originator: The original Gold Ribbed Hare's Ear has been in use for over 100 years. **Variant:** Nigel Dennis, SA.
Hook: Size 10, **12**, **14**, 16 Tiemco 3761 or similar 2× long, heavy wire nymph hook.
Thread: 6/0 brown.
Tail: Brown partridge hackle fibres.
Abdomen: Dubbing mix: 70% dark fur from natural hare's mask, 20% dark olive hare's fur, 5% brown Antron, 5% olive Antron. Dub sparsely to form 'carrot-shaped' taper.
Rib: Fine gold wire.
Thorax: Same mix as abdomen, dubbed thick to produce pronounced bulge. Include plenty of spiky guard hair.
Wing case: 4 to 8 strands Holographic tinsel (depending on size of fly).
Weight and Hackle: None
Tying tips: It can be difficult to obtain whole hare's masks in this country – I import mine half a dozen at a time from overseas. The hare's fur sold in packets is far less effective, and tends to be too light in colour. If you tie this pattern correctly, it should look like a spiky, scruffy mess – and the trout just love it!
Commercially tied alternatives: Both the traditional Gold Ribbed Hare's Ear and Flash-back Hare's Ears are available commercially. However, they are often tied too neatly (otherwise you probably would not buy them!) and are usually lighter in colour than I prefer.
When and how to fish this pattern: I regard this as the ultimate generic small stillwater nymph. It imitates mayfly nymphs, caddis pupae and larvae, hatching midge pupae, small damsel nymphs – and who knows what else. I believe the Holographic tinsel flash back is an important trigger mimicking the air bubble that many nymphs and pupae develop prior to hatching. The addition of Antron to the dubbing mix gives this pattern transluscence and a subtle sparkle. Deadly all year fished with a slow hand twist on a floating line.

DDD AND BLACK DDD

Originator: Tom Sutcliffe, SA. Black DDD **Variant:** Nigel Dennis, SA.
Hook: Size: **8**, **10**, **12**, **14**, 16 The standard tying uses a dry fly hook, but I prefer a 1× heavy wet fly such as the Tiemco 9300, to give a better chance of pulling a big fish out of weedy water.
Thread: 6/0 brown, or 3/0 brown Monocord for larger sizes.
Tail: Klipspringer or deer hair.
Body: Klipspringer or deer hair.
Legs: Single strand pearl Krystal Flash tied to form 'V'.
Hackle: Brown cock hackle, or spun collar of klipspringer or deer hair (I prefer the latter - or a mixture of hackle and spun hair).
Tying tip: Trim body to form carrot shape. Tie in extra tail fibres as you are sure to clip off a few when trimming the body. The Black DDD is tied using black deer hair for the body and sparse black cock hackle for the tail and collar hackle. The 'legs' are a single strand of brown Krystal Flash. I trim this variant to an oval beetle-like shape. I find the black version most effective in small sizes, 12, 14 and 16.
Commercially tied alternatives: The DDD is such a widely used fly that all fly tackle dealers will carry them – although if you want the black version you will almost certainly have to tie them yourself!
When and how to fish this pattern: The standard DDD is an excellent generic dry searching pattern. No one is really sure what it represents – perhaps a drowned grasshopper having a bad hair day! The Black DDD works well for me when beetles and other small terrestrials are on the water; in my experience it regularly out-performs 'proper' beetle imitations such as the Foam Beetle. It is also a passable floating snail imitation. Both patterns are effective year-round.

VARIEGATED CHENILLE WOOLLY BUGGER

Originator: Russell Blessing USA.
Hook: Size **8**, 10 Tiemco 3761 or similar 2× long, heavy wire nymph hook.
Thread: 6/0 black.
Tail: Black turkey marabou.
Body: Black/brown variegated chenille, wound to form fat body.
Hackle: Black genetic hen capes are best, as the hackles are longer and more webby.
Rib: Fine gold wire (wound in opposite direction to hackle).
Head: (optional) Gold metal bead or black glass bead.
Weight: (optional) Up to 8 turns lead wire. I generally use unweighted Woolly Buggers on a sunk line, and bead head or weighted versions with a floating line.
Tying tip: Select the soft, feathery marabou fibres from base of feather for the tail. These are far more mobile than the stiffer fibres at the tip of a marabou plume. An olive variant is also very effective using green/brown variegated chenille for the body, and olive or black hackle and tail. An all-orange Woolly Bugger can work wonders in winter.
Commercially tied alternatives: Black Woolly Buggers are widely available and you should find patterns fairly similar to my tying in most tackle shops.
When and how to fish this pattern: Probably the best-ever generic large searching pattern; effective just about anywhere anytime. I believe the Variegated Chenille Woolly Bugger most closely imitates the aeschnid dragonfly nymph – but trout may mistake it for any large food item, perhaps even a swimming frog! Fish on any appropriate line (depending on depth) using a jerky hand twist, various strip retrieves or ripping it back.

VINYL DAMSEL NYMPH

Originator: Nigel Dennis, SA.
Hook: Size 8, **10**, 12 Tiemco 3761. Gently bend hook shank up with pliers at approx 30°, one-third along from eye (you will need to do this carefully as the hook shank may snap if too much pressure is applied). Alternatively, use a Swimming Larva Hook, such as the Daiichi 1870.
Thread: 6/0 brown or dark olive.
Tail: Olive turkey marabou.
Underbody: Olive marabou (wound as herl – not dubbed).
Overbody/Rib: Olive vinyl tube or vinyl V-rib in not-quite touching turns.
Thorax: Olive hare's fur mixed with a little olive SLF for sparkle.
Hackle: Olive-dyed partridge.
Wing case: Brown-mottled turkey, treated with Dave's Flexament for durability.
Eyes: Black-burnt mono, or small black bead eyes on mono stalk.
Weight: 4 to 8 turns lead wire wound along bent section of hook shank (essential to ensure the damsel swims the right way up!).
Tying tip: A rather complex pattern, but the results justify the effort! As with the Woolly Bugger, select soft, feathery marabou plume for the tail to ensure a lively mobile fly. I believe the translucent vinyl-rib and realistic partridge hackle legs are also important trigger factors.
Commercially tied alternative: Hugh Huntley's Red Eye Damsel.
When and how to fish this pattern: Damsel nymphs are most active in spring and early summer. I catch fish on this pattern throughout the year, but find the small sizes best in winter. Fish with a slow to jerky hand twist on floating and intermediate lines.

It doesn't get much better than this! Here I am dead-drifting a small nymph through a shallow run in a pretty stream. Stealth is vital when wading small streams. You often end the day with sore knees, backache, and a few cuts and scratches – but it's all part of the game.

River trout and stillwater trout behave very differently. So differently, in fact, that it is rather like fishing for another species altogether. I find this refreshing, and while many anglers tend to lean heavily towards either stillwater or river fishing, I enjoy both, and believe that there are at least a couple of instances in each case when trout fly-fishing is elevated to the sublime. One is fishing a dam from the freedom of a kick boat; the other is wading a small stream and delicately casting a nymph or dry fly upstream to likely trout lies.

There is a general perception that fishing rivers is more difficult than stillwater fishing. For the absolute beginner, I would agree that it probably is. At least your line stays put on a dam, and doesn't go belting away in a strong current. And when fishing a dam, it is possible to make a real hash of casting, and yet still catch the occasional fish. A stillwater trout may cruise into your area *after* the splashy cast. If you pound a bad cast on top of a trout holding in a lie in a river, it will spook – and probably spend the next hour hiding under the nearest rock.

An angler experienced in both disciplines, however, might well say that rivers are easier to predict and understand. I expect to make several visits to a new dam before I get a feel for the place. If it is a very big dam, it may require many days of fishing before I really get a good idea of where the trout are and what they are doing.

Once you have mastered the basics, though, a river can be read like a book. Get this right, and it is not unusual to have instant success (I'm talking about fishing a section of river you have never set eyes upon before and getting into a fish within five minutes – or maybe even on the very first cast).

Before we look at the tricks and techniques for reading rivers and fishing them effectively, there are a couple of mind-set adjustments necessary for this branch of the sport.

Firstly, if you have mainly fished still waters, you are going to find river trout a bit on the small side. On a good dam, a 2-pounder would barely warrant a second glance. Prime trophy still waters may hold trout that *average* 6 pounds or more; on most South African rivers, a 2-pounder would be a very nice fish – and the average catch might only be 8 ounces or so. Once you get used to the difference in size, small river trout can be as much fun as the monsters that live in dams. I get just as excited about a 2-pounder from a river as I do when I catch a stillwater 5-pounder.

Secondly – and many stillwater anglers grumble about this – you *are* going to lose more flies when river fishing. On overgrown small streams especially, there are infinite opportunities to hang flies up in trees and bushes on the back cast – usually just out of your reach.

When deep nymphing, it is also common to snag on rocks on the bottom. Over the years, I have learned how to deal with these inconveniences so that they not longer spoil my enjoyment of river fishing.

I think it would be pertinent at this point to briefly examine the differences between our two trout species – **browns** and **rainbows**. In wild-spawning populations, where both species have been introduced over the years, it is usual to find that one species eventually becomes dominant. In the majority of South Africa's streams, rainbow trout predominate. Nonetheless, browns are generally considered to be the wilier of the two, and are therefore much harder to catch. In my experience, though, this seems to vary

Worldwide, browns are regarded as being more wily than rainbows. In my experience, a great deal depends on river itself. This Lower Mooi brown positively whacked a Peacock Woolly Worm.

depending on the nature of the stream. My local KwaZulu-Natal brown trout streams – such as the Bushmans and Mooi Rivers – are not especially difficult as they are fairly substantial rivers. However, the Witte River in the Western Cape is a notoriously challenging brown trout river –

A light 2-weight outfit and a dry fly is an excellent way to tackle the free-rising trout in a small high-altitude stream. The tiny pockets and pools may hold rather small trout (mainly 8 to 10 inches), but fishing such water is a lot of fun.

A waterfall plunge pool is an obvious place to try for a large river trout. However, on rivers where trout are heavily 'harvested', such spots soon become fished out – so you may need to seek out more inaccessible places to find the better fish.

possibly because it is such a tiny, crystal-clear stream.

The only opportunity I have had to directly compare the two species was on the Kwaai River north of Plettenberg Bay; this fragile little brook is a rarity in that it holds browns and rainbows. Both species were so easily spooked that it was a battle to catch anything at all! It seems to me, then, that the difficulty lies not in the species of trout present, but rather in the size, flow and clarity of the stream in question.

Where browns do differ is that when they get spooked they often hide for a long time – sometimes for the rest of the day. So, if another angler has fished through the waters of a brown trout stream a few hours previously, you are probably wasting your time. Rainbows generally recover more quickly from a fright, and resume feeding after an hour or two.

I recall a trip to the Upper Karringmelkspruit a few years ago. This pretty Karoo rainbow trout stream was pitifully low when I visited it (I think the flow was equivalent to about three hosepipes!). I had managed to catch plenty of small fish up to a pound or so, when I spotted a really nice rainbow holding at the head of a large undercut cliff pool. I dead-drifted a Hare's Ear nymph over the trout, and got a take on the very first cast – which I somehow managed to miss. I decided to rest the pool, and returned an hour later and got the same fish, again on the first cast. At just over 3 pounds, it was easily the best from the entire trip. Had I been fishing brown trout water, then I would bet money that, on having missed and spooked it on the first try, it would have spent the rest of the day hiding under a rock.

LOCATING THE SWEET SPOTS

The basics for locating river trout are similar to those of stillwater fish, i.e. the trout's need for food, shelter from predators and, during hot weather, cool, well-oxygenated water. In the case of rivers, however, there is a fourth factor in the equation, and that is current. Current is the conveyor belt that brings food to river trout. Unlike stillwater trout that must cruise to hunt down food, river trout hold position in a lie and wait for the current to bring their food to them. It requires a considerable energy investment for a trout to hold position in fast water – to the extent that a trout may burn more calories fighting a strong current than it might gain in food intake. Very sensibly, our quarry uses the pockets and seams of slower water as a holding lie from which it will dash out and grab passing food from the main flow. Learn to read the water for prime holding lies, and you are well on the way to catching lots of river trout.

Pools

River pools create a prime lie, as they supply lots of food as well as shelter from current and predators. Fish the edge of the main current tongue as it enters the pool, or where the current starts to peter out, and you will probably be fishing over the best trout in the pool. Trout may also hold in the slow, deep water back in the main part of the pool, but these are unlikely to be the larger fish; less current means less food passing their way. The exception to this rule is when a big hatch of mayfly or caddis is underway. At these times, when food is abundant, it is worth the trout's while to fight faster water. During an evening rise, big fish commonly drop down to the shallow tail of the pool, where the current speeds up.

Runs

Runs occur where the river narrows and flow increases. The chances are that a run may be fairly deep as well. A fast run with little to break the water flow is unlikely to hold many fish – too much energy is needed to fight the flow for too little reward. However, given some fair-sized boulders or rock sills (which create pockets of calmer water on the riverbed), a run can become highly productive. I have (in several rivers) caught larger trout from deep runs with structure than I have from pools. And many anglers think that the big pools will always hold the best fish!

Riffles

A riffle is characterised by fairly shallow water flowing swiftly over a pebbled bed. It may not look like good trout habitat, but add a few larger rocks or depressions in the riverbed (these cushion the flow), and a riffle can hold lots of fish. The choppy broken water surface hides trout from predators, but also makes it exceedingly difficult for us to spot the fish. On the plus side, trout in choppy water experience a distorted view of the outside world, allowing the angler a close approach.

Surprisingly, riffles are very rich in insect life as the tiny spaces between pebbles create perfect homes for huge numbers of mayfly nymphs and caddis larvae. Riffles mostly hold small to average-sized fish, but during a big insect hatch, or when oxygen demand is high in hot weather, some good-sized trout may move into this type of water.

A jumble of tiny pools and runs is typical of a high-altitude stream running off a steep gradient. Such 'pocket water' is best fished using a very short cast, keeping the rod high to avoid drag.

Pocket water

Rivers flowing through terrain with a moderate gradient generally show the classic riffle, run and pool structure.

Tilt the geology, and we see pocket water typical of the upper reaches of many streams in mountainous terrain. Here the river plunges over a bed of huge boulders, rock sills and stones. Often there will be a small waterfall or two thrown in – just to make it all look pretty.

In pocket water, trout will hold in the jumble of tiny pools and runs. Frequently, trout lies will be no larger than your kitchen sink, and a *big* pool in pocket water may only be the size of a bathtub. While pocket water holds plenty of fish, many of them may be small. Nonetheless, it is fun to fish; just treat it like any other stream, and search out the lies on the edge of the main current – even though, in this instance, it may be a case of picking up trout in a tiny, foot-square holding area. Anything short of a white-water torrent is probably worth a cast or two in pocket water.

Canal water

The other extreme is sometimes found at the bottom end of what can be considered viable trout water – the low-altitude meadow reaches, where you might also catch yellowfish and bass. Canal water is deep and slow. Locating trout in these sluggish, muddy-bottomed, rather uninspiring stretches can be difficult. There is little in the way of current flow to indicate trout lies, but if you search out bends, sunken logs or overhanging trees, you may be able to make some sense of it all. The reward for slow, patient fishing may be the largest trout you are ever likely to catch in a South African river.

Bank water

Just as stillwater anglers often mistakenly imagine that the best fish are always far out in the deepest part of a dam, it is easy to miss many opportunities by fishing only the middle of a river. Good holding and feeding lies are often found right against the bank. The water may only be knee deep, but if there is some cover from overhanging bushes or tall grass, there is a good chance that a trout will be in residence. And where the current has undercut a bank, you could have a prime holding area. A deep undercut bend pool with moderate current is a fine example. Add a tangle of tree roots in the undercut, and it will be the kind of place that would make a big brown trout very happy. Of course you don't need three guesses to figure out where that big brown will head the moment you hook into it!

Seasonal migrations

A final word or two on locating trout in rivers. Some streams experience seasonal trout migrations, usually brought about by thermal needs and/or the urge to breed. The lower reaches of some trout streams become uncomfortably warm in mid- to late summer, so trout may seek out cooler water in the high-altitude headwaters. Likewise, the lower river may have few clean gravel areas for spawning – often caused by silt from agricultural erosion smothering the gravel beds –

Dam fishers may need to make a mind-set adjustment when they tackle trout in small rivers, where the average fish may only weigh 6 ounces. Larger fertile rivers can produce plenty of fish in the 12-ounce to 1$\frac{1}{2}$-pound range, but a 3-pounder would be trophy size.

Deep, slow-flowing 'canal water' sometimes grows the largest of the river catchment trout, and patient, deep fishing can pay off. This run is more than 8 feet deep and I was hoping for a nice one, but when my strike indicator zipped away, it turned out to be only a 10-ouncer!

and as the spawning season approaches, trout will attempt to reach the more pristine tributaries or upper reaches of the main river to breed.

Migration is a significant factor in some river systems and entirely absent in others. Knowledge built up over the years can be a big help in deciding when and where to fish. My local river, the Mooi, is a good example. The Mooi itself experiences little trout movement, as a number of high waterfalls along the river block migration. The Mooi's main tributary – appropriately named the Little Mooi – is a different story altogether, as there are long stretches without barrier waterfalls.

The headwaters of the Little Mooi are reduced to a trickle at the end of a dry winter, so come the opening of the trout season in September, the headwaters are largely a waste of time for fishing, and hold only a few thin 8- to 10-inch browns. However, by December, given good rainfall and some hot weather, those same upper reaches can be full of nice trout that have moved up from the slow, warmer waters many kilometres downstream.

A second migration starts in late April, and this tiny stream – in places only a rod-length wide – receives an additional injection of large wild brown trout seeking out clean gravel on which to spawn.

PRESENTATION

Nature has been kind to us when it comes to fishing for river trout. Firstly, trout always lie facing into a current; this eliminates the big unknown factor in dam fishing, where a trout might cruise in any direction. Secondly, although trout have a wide field of vision, they do have a blind spot that extends behind them. This means you can say for certain which way a river trout will be facing *and* utilise the blind spot to creep up on it undetected.

The principal technique for fishing the small to medium-sized streams that constitute the majority of South African river fishing, therefore, is to cast upstream. There are occasions where downstream fishing is called for, but I regard this as a minor tactic, one which we will examine briefly later in this chapter.

Before we move on to specific tactics, I'd like say a few words on tackle for river fishing. Back in the 1960s and '70s, I mostly fished small streams in England, and I exclusively used a 7½-foot 5 weight (which was considered a light

The turbulent currents of this miniature waterfall allowed me to make a very close approach and fish a very short line to avoid drag on my team of weighted nymphs.

outfit at the time!). A short rod on a small stream had a kind of symmetry to it that seemed to make sense. Of late, I have changed my thinking. On tiny streams, I now fish an 8-foot 4-inch 2 weight. For anything from a medium-sized stream up, I prefer my 9-foot 4 weight. The extra length gives better line control, and is easier to roll cast – along with some of the other fancy casts we will get onto in a moment. I overline my 4 weight on rivers by using a 5 weight double-taper floating line. Going one line size up loads the rod better at short range, and also makes it easier to chuck heavily weighted nymphs.

DRY-FLY TACTICS

Dry-fly tactics are consistently effective on most fast and shallow South African streams and rivers. This is the most straightforward river-fishing technique – plus, of course, you get the added fun of watching a trout actually eat the fly. Even when there is no fly hatch it is often possible to fish through likely holding lies and entice a trout to the surface with an attractor dry fly. The highly visible Humpy is an excellent example. Keep a low profile and steadily work your way upstream, firing short casts directly upstream or up and across the water. As long as you keep a low profile on the bank or slowly wade upstream, most stream fishing only requires casts in the 5- to 10-yard range.

All this sounds very easy. Indeed, it would be, if it were not for that great obstacle facing all river fishers, namely, *drag*. Drag occurs when you cast across currents of varying speeds. In its most extreme form, conflicting currents will form a bow in the line and make the fly 'motor boat' across the stream, creating a big 'V' wake. Trout do not like this. It may put them down entirely, or at the very least, cause them to be wary of subsequent presentations, even if you manage to make the next cast drag free. Even a tiny amount of drag on the fly – known as micro drag – can result in a refusal by the trout. This is the toughest challenge facing river fishers, so let's take a look at ways to overcome the problem.

The simplest method to ensure a drag-free drift is to cast directly upstream, thus covering water with a constant flow. Usually, this means wading the stream to get into the right casting position. The direct upstream cast works well in riffles and pocket water, as the choppy currents mask the disturbance made by the fly line falling on the water. Bear in mind that you will be casting right over the backs of the trout that you are hoping to catch. Without a good ripple on the water it is likely you will 'line' a trout and spook it. Consequently, this technique is not effective in the calmer runs and pools.

Let's say you have fast water close in, but want to present a fly right on the slower current seam a little further out, where you reckon a trout could be holding. This is a classic situation for major-league drag. That fast water will grab the line and, within a couple of seconds into the drift, the fly will be skating horribly across the surface. The best way to solve the problem is to make your fly line do the opposite of the pull of the current, by using a **reach-mend** cast. If you can make a simple overhead cast, then you can do a reach mend – it's easy. On the forward stroke, instead of pointing the rod in the direction of the cast as you shoot line, tilt the rod upstream right across your body, so that it is horizontal with the water. The result is a nice, *upstream* curve in the line. This will gain several seconds of drag-free float before the fast current takes up the slack. You can buy yourself more time by adding *on-the-water mends* to the line. These are like mini roll casts. Make a circular motion with the rod tip to flick the line belly upstream. You may need to make these corrections several times during a drift. Given the opposite situation – slow water in close and an interesting, fishy-looking edge to fast water further out – a downstream reach cast is necessary to create a *downstream* belly in the line. If this sounds a bit complicated, remember that all you need to do is anticipate the flow and throw line mends that are the *opposite* of what the current is going to do to your line.

Still on the drag problem ... there are a few additional tricks to prolong a drag-free float. One is to shorten the leader, but add a much longer tippet. The tippet is likely to land in a heap of coils, so it will take a few moments for the line to tighten up and pull the tippet straight. This can add several precious seconds before the dry fly skates.

Conflicting currents are common on many of our faster streams. Currents can be so convoluted and complex that a simple up-, or downstream mend will not overcome drag. More 'get-out-of-trouble' tricks include the **wiggle** and **puddle casts**. To make a wiggle cast, shake the rod tip from side to side as you shoot line. This causes the line to fall in snaking curves on the water. To perform a puddle cast, simply drop the rod tip right to the water as you shoot line. The result is, again, a snaky line that allows the dry fly to bob along naturally in the current – for a while at least.

Dry-fly selection

I have had quite a lot to say about location and presentation, and very little so far about dry-fly selection. This is because river trout are generally even less selective than stillwater fish; they have only a moment to decide if a floating item looks like food, and to grab it before the current whisks it away.

I find I can get away with three dry-fly patterns on most streams. As I mentioned earlier, the Humpy is an excellent big attractor fly in choppy water, or when no fish are rising. Given a caddis hatch, the Elk Hair Caddis seldom fails, although it can also be a good searching pattern. Most

In some streams, deep holding water has been created by the construction of artificial weirs. Such changes to the watercourse can, however, cause environmental problems, such as silting and warming of the water, endangering the trout's prime habitat.

GETAWAY GUIDE TO FLY-FISHING IN SOUTH AFRICA

mayflies are very effectively imitated with the Parachute
Adams – simply vary the size so that it roughly matches that
of the insects on the water.

UPSTREAM NYMPH TACTICS

Dry-fly fishing on rivers is a lot of fun, but I actually prefer
to fish a nymph. Certainly you miss out on the excitement
of watching a trout engulf the fly on the surface, but I get
just as much of a buzz from seeing my strike indicator zip
away when pulled by some unseen force. Nymphing probes
the mysterious depths of a stream, getting a fly down into
those dark corners and deep swirling currents that may hold
a big old fish – the kind of trout that is unlikely to rise to a
delicately presented size 16 dry fly.

Nymphing a river is, I believe, the more technically
demanding of the two approaches. Dry-fly fishing essentially
operates in two dimensions. You are working only on the
surface, so the challenge is about getting the fly to drift into
the trout's field of vision without
spooking it and, of course,
avoiding the dreaded drag.
Nymphing works in three,
or rather, in a sense, four
dimensions. You have the
complication of depth – the third
dimension – and time, in the form of current velocity, gives
a fourth dimension to this style of fishing.

You need to be able to read the river's flow in order to
be able to anticipate how far upstream to cast a nymph rig

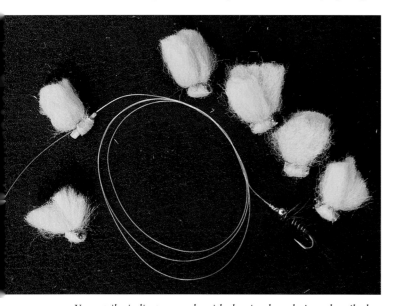

*Yarn strike indicators made with the simple technique described
on the opposite page. These indicators can be positioned
anywhere on the leader or tippet in a matter of seconds.*

in order to achieve the necessary depth of presentation over
a likely trout lie.

Before we move onto modern strike-indicator/leaded-fly
nymphing, I want to talk briefly about the way we used to
fish nymphs back in the old days, i.e., **traditional upstream
nymphing**. This method of nymphing still has its place –
especially if you manage to spot a trout holding in the
current. Tie on a small, lightly weighted nymph (a Flashback
Hare's Ear is usually my first choice). Use a tapered mono
leader and 4× or 5× fluorocarbon tippet treated with
floatant down to within 2 feet of the fly. Cast upstream
of the fish, and allow the nymph to dead-drift back in line
with the trout. Now, unlike a take on a dry fly, trout may
inhale and eject a nymph very rapidly. This is where you
need to *watch* very carefully indeed. If you see the tippet
or leader pause or stab forward – strike! Likewise, if the
trout moves position when you guess your nymph to be close
by – strike! If you see the trout's mouth flash white as it
opens – strike! In fact, if you even *suspect* that the trout may
have taken the fly, strike anyway, as you will probably only
get one shot at this.

After three of four drifts past the fish without a reaction
you can try the **induced take** tactic. When you judge the fly
to be about 2 feet in front of the trout, raise the rod tip
slightly to cause the fly to lift a few inches in the water and
then allow the fly to continue the dead-drift towards the fish.
This method is exceptionally effective, and caught hundreds
of chalkstream trout for me back in the UK.

Traditional upstream nymphing is a good choice when
you can sight fish. Hence, it is ideally suited to the English
chalkstreams and American spring creeks. While we do get
some opportunities to sight fish with a nymph here in South
Africa, many of our streams do not have sufficient clarity, or
have such turbulent currents that often it is impossible to see
trout in the water. This is where the modern strike indicator
and heavily weighted nymph style really scores. It allows you
to get down deep in strong currents, and easily detect takes
that would mostly go unnoticed if you were relying on
watching your leader or tip of the fly line for bite indication.

The setup for **deep nymphing** goes like this. Short tapered
leader – mono or fluorocarbon – cut back to about 6 feet,
and a 4-foot tippet of 4× or 5× fluorocarbon.

At the business end of the rig, tie on a heavily weighted
fly. The Peacock Woolly Worm in size 12 or Heavy Half Back
size 14 are both excellent. A second fly is added by tying
onto the bend of the first – 'New Zealand-style'. A distance
of 18 inches to 2 feet is usually about right – much closer
than you would space flies for dam fishing. The point fly is

The Bushmans River near Giant's Castle is regarded as one of South Africa's finest brown trout streams. Fish average about 10 ounces, although a few wily old monsters lurk in some of the deepest pools. Nymphs and dry flies can be effectively fished upstream in the crystal-clear water.

much smaller, and can be lightly weighted or entirely unweighted. I usually go for a Spring Creek Pheasant Tail, or my 'old faithful' Flashback Hare's Ear in size 16, or 18 if the water is exceptionally clear.

Now we come to the essential part of the rig – the **strike indicator**. Lots of options are available. Floating putty works okay, but it makes a bit of a splash; also, strong currents often pull it under. Stick-on foam indicators work pretty well, but are difficult to move on the leader. The Americans like the small polystyrene bobbers, but I find these rather clunky. The last option is the tried-and-trusted brightly coloured yarn. Yarn treated with silicone floatant stays buoyant for ages, it's light (so it doesn't interfere with casting too much) and it is generally, and by far, I believe, the best choice.

The standard way to fish a yarn indicator is to knot it onto the leader. There are a number of special knots by which this can be accomplished, but when you want to move the indicator on the line, you have to undo the knot and tie another, and this tends to leave kinks in the leader. Too much hassle for me! Here is a great little idea for strike

indicators that I found on a fly-fishing website. Take a thin piece of light plastic tubing (the stuff you get from cotton ear buds is perfect). Loop a piece of yarn over the tube; pinch the yarn, and secure it with several turns of tying thread. Apply a smear of five-minute epoxy to the tubing to stop the yarn from sliding off. Clip the tubing close to the yarn, and your indicator is complete. Thread the indicator on the tippet before you tie on the flies. To secure the indicator on the line, simply push a short piece of toothpick into the tube. The beauty of this system is that you can place the indicator anywhere on the tippet or leader, and it only takes a second to move it – by removing the toothpick and sliding the indicator to where you want it. I use orange yarn most of the time, although on heavily fished rivers, trout may become wary of brightly coloured indicators. It is worth making up some white, grey, or even black yarn indicators as well, in case you encounter this situation.

The technique for fishing this rig is similar to that used for upstream dry-fly fishing. A dead-drift is important, so all the drag-defeating tricks covered in the dry-fly section apply. Most of the time, the indicator is best set at one-and-a-half times the

When fishing for skittish trout in a tiny brook, it pays to make use of all available cover. I quietly slid into position, using shade and vegetation as cover, to cast a lightly weighted nymph rig. The white strike indicator is approaching a deeply undercut pool – a classic lie for a good fish.

water depth, going up to twice the depth in very fast water. This means constant adjustments to the strike indicator on the leader. You might be fishing a 2-foot deep riffle one moment, and 30 yards upstream need to get deep down into 8 feet of water in a run or pool. During an average morning's fishing, I would expect to adjust the indicator depth a couple of dozen times. Takes can vary from a slight hesitation in the indicator to it zipping away under the surface. You will, of course, need to strip back line to avoid slack, and strike *instantly* at any suspicious movement of the indicator.

Ideally, you should try to present the flies about a foot off the bottom. If very strong currents prevent you from getting depth, try a really heavy 'bomber' of a fly, like the Soft Hackle Woolly Worm – I tie this with up to 30 turns of lead wire wound around the shank. You can also add weight in the form of split shot or Deep Soft Weight placed about a foot above the dropper fly. Such rigs are a bit like trying to cast a brick, and require a slow, lazy stroke and a wide casting loop. As a general rule, if you are not getting takes, try setting the strike indicator a little deeper. If you find you are constantly getting hung up on the bottom, move the indicator a bit closer to the flies.

If you are getting few takes by dead-drifting the nymph, it is worth experimenting by agitating the fly. Give the odd quick strip as you retrieve the line coming back towards you. Also, at the end of a drift, instead of lifting off to make another cast, hold the rod high for a few seconds; this will cause the team of nymphs to rise up in the water. In my experience, agitating nymphs works best when there is a little colour in the water. It can also be effective when trout are actively hunting down caddis pupa and mayfly nymphs just prior to a hatch.

FISHING DOWNSTREAM

At times, nature will conspire to make it impossible to fish upstream. Thick bank-side bushes with water too deep to wade would be a typical example. When fishing downstream, a longer than normal cast will be needed so that the trout don't see you (remember, trout always face into the current so they will be staring straight at you). A careful stealthy approach is essential – particularly if the water is very clear. Also, put plenty of slack into the line using the wiggle or puddle casts. You can also feed out slack to prolong the drift. These techniques can allow either a dry fly or nymph and

The lower reaches of our trout streams are frequently discoloured by agricultural run-off. Dead-drifted presentations are less effective under these conditions, so it often pays to swing a team of wet flies or a streamer pattern across the current to attract the trout's attention.

indicator rig to drift into otherwise impossible-to-reach fishy places, such as runs covered by a tunnel of overhanging trees.

Other styles incorporate the downstream cast as the prime method of fishing. These are **traditional wet fly-fishing** and **streamer techniques**. The downstream wet fly is a centuries-old tactic. A team of flies – you can use lightly weighted nymphs, or the traditional winged wet fly or spider patterns – is cast downstream and across. The current swings the flies around so that they finish up below you. You can give the flies a little action by twitching the rod tip, or simply let the current impart the necessary action; often the latter is best. Takes are felt by a firm tug on the line.

Wet flies work well in riffles and other shallow water, but are less effective in very deep pools and runs as it is difficult to get the flies down deep. Wet flies frequently out-fish dead-drift upstream nymphs when the water is beginning to clear after rain; the cross-current swing seems to get the trout's attention when a dead-drifted fly may go unnoticed.

Streamer fishing is similar, except you actively work the fly by stripping it back. You will recall that I am not fond of the fast 2-foot strip retrieve in dams, but on rivers it seems to work very well. Streamers can be heavily weighted, and my favourite

is the Soft Hackle Woolly Worm tied with 20 to 30 turns of lead wire around the body. Bead Head Woolly Buggers and Mrs Simpsons are also effective river streamer patterns (in the case of the latter it could be that it makes a passable imitation of the freshwater crab, a common food source for trout in many South African rivers). The advantage of streamer fishing is that drag is not an issue, as you are actively retrieving the fly. Floating lines and weighted streamers gain sufficient depth in most situations, but in very strong currents you might need to go to a very fast sink Hi D for a deep presentation.

Generally, trout take a streamer first or second cast, or not at all, so it pays to work through the water quickly. Fire a couple of casts to each likely spot, and if you don't get a take, move on. This makes streamer fishing an effective way of prospecting the lower reaches of trout rivers with a scattered small population of what will very likely be larger-than-average fish. In less than ideal conditions, i.e. when faced with discoloured water from storm run-off, fishing a large, high-visibility streamer is also a good bet.

SPRING CREEK PHEASANT TAIL NYMPH

Originator: Frank Sawyer, UK. Differs considerably from the original Sawyer Pheasant Tail Nymph, but has proved its worth on the American spring creeks – some of the hardest-fished catch-and-release waters in the world.

Hook: Size 20, **18**, **16**, 14, 2× long, heavy-wire nymph hook.

Weight: None, or 2 turns lead wire around the thorax.

Thread: Brown 8/0.

Tail: 3 or 4 fibres of pheasant tail.

Abdomen: Pheasant tail fibres wound to form slim carrot-shaped taper.

Rib: Very fine copper wire.

Thorax: Dubbed hare's ear.

Flashback: Gold Mylar size 14.

Tying tips: Keep the entire fly slim and understated.

Commercially tied alternatives: You will be lucky to find this exact variation in the shops, but standard Pheasant Tail Nymphs are readily available.

When and how to fish this pattern: For many years I regarded the Pheasant Tail as an inferior pattern to the Hare's Ear – that is, *until* I started using it in very small sizes (16s and 18s). It very effectively imitates many of the smaller species of mayfly nymph. A Spring Creek PTN is best fished teamed with a heavily weighted pattern, fished upstream dead-drift. In very clear water, this fly has often taken the best fish of the day for me.

PARACHUTE ADAMS

Originator: Len Halliday, USA.

Hook: 20, 18, **16**, **14**, 12, standard dry-fly hook.

Tail: Grizzly and brown hackle fibres mixed.

Thread: Brown 8/0.

Body: 'Adams' grey Superfine dubbing.

Wing post: White calf (standard dressing). I prefer dun Z-Lon for its translucence, or orange Poly yarn for a high-visibility version.

Hackle: Grizzly and brown genetic cock hackle.

Tying tips: Tie up a few sparsely hackled flies for fishing calm pools; these will also be very useful on dams during a mayfly hatch. I also tie a densely hackled version to ride through rough water (use the orange Poly yarn wing post for these, so you can keep sight of the fly as it bobs along in a choppy riffle). Useful variants include a black-bodied Adams, favoured by guide Fred Steynberg for the Rhodes streams. During a Sulphur mayfly hatch, I have done well using a body of yellow Superfine dubbing, and cream/ginger tail and hackle.

Commercially tied alternatives: The standard Adams is one of the world's most popular dry flies, and all fly shops should carry them. You might have to search around a bit to find the Parachute version, though.

When and how to fish this pattern: Probably the best generic mayfly imitation ever devised. The low-floating Parachute Adams can imitate both the dun and spinner stages of the insect. Match the size of fly to the naturals on the water and fish with the standard upstream dry-fly techniques.

VINYL CADDIS PUPA

Originator: Bill Logan, UK.

Hook: 16, **14**, 12, Kamazan B110 or similar heavy-wire, curved caddis hook.

Weight: None.

Thread: 6/0 brown.

Tail: None.

Underbody: Gold Mylar, ribbed with very sparse hare dubbing to make it a bit less 'flashy'.

Rib: Olive vinyl tubing in not-quite-touching turns.

Herl: Natural ostrich wound between turns of vinyl-rib.

Antennae: Two strands of pearl Krystal Flash.

Hackle: Brown partridge (very sparse).

Collar: Peacock herl.

Head: Small gold bead.

Tying tips: This is not a difficult pattern to master, just a little time consuming due to the complexity and number of materials used. You can vary the underbody and rib colours to imitate different caddis species. A pearl Mylar underbody, with dark olive rib and green peacock as the herl also looks great and works well.

Commercially tied alternatives: I have not seen this tying of the Vinyl Caddis Pupa in the shops as yet. Fur-bodied caddis pupae can be obtained, but in my experience, they are far less effective than this pattern.

When and how to fish this pattern: Fish this fly any time you see caddis on the water – it is deadly! During a caddis hatch fish the Vinyl Caddis Pupa under a dry Elk Hair Caddis as a 'hedged bet'. A good deep-searching fly at other times fished with the standard upstream strike indicator method.

FLASHBACK HARE'S EAR

Originator: The original Gold Ribbed Hare's Ear has been in use for over 100 years. The Flashback style of nymph is generally thought to have originated in the UK.

Hook: Size **16**, **14**, 12 Tiemco 3761 or similar 2× long, heavy-wire nymph hook.

Weight: 3 to 8 turns lead wire.

Thread: 6/0 brown.

Tail: Brown partridge hackle fibres, or guard hair from hare's mask.

Abdomen: Dubbing mix: 70% dark fur from natural hare's mask, 20% dark olive hare's fur, 5% brown Antron, 5% olive Antron. Dub sparsely to form carrot-shaped taper.

Rib: Fine gold wire.

Thorax: Same mix as abdomen, dubbed thick to produce a pronounced bulge. Include plenty of spiky guard hair.

Wingcase: Gold Mylar.

Tying tips: The trick with all hare's ear patterns is to get a buggy, spiky look. This is more a style of fly than a definitive dressing. Black Hare's Ears are also excellent river patterns – use black-dyed rabbit or hare dubbing. If you suspect the presence of yellow stonefly nymphs (rather rare, but present in some high-altitude waters), then an all yellow version incorporating yellow-dyed rabbit fur is worth a try.

Commercially tied alternatives: Flashback Hare's Ear patterns are tied commercially, but generally the colour is lighter than I prefer, and often they are unweighted.

When and how to fish this pattern: I make no apologies for including the Hare's Ear in both the stillwater and river fly selections – this fly seems to work on most trout waters just about anywhere in the world! The river version is moderately weighted and incorporates a gold flashback. For reasons that only the fish understand, I find the gold flashback better than the Holographic tinsel version for stream trout. This pattern is my first choice when sight fishing for trout holding in shallow water. Also excellent as a point fly when searching deep runs and pools. The standard upstream dead-drift method is usually best.

SOFT HACKLE WOOLLY WORM
Originator: Rick Ostoff, USA.
Hook: 10, 8, Tiemco 3761 or similar 2× long, heavy-wire nymph hook.
Weight: 20 to 30 turns lead wire.
Thread: 6/0 black.
Tail: Tuft of black rabbit fur cut from Zonker strip.
Tag: Scarlet floss silk.
Body: 90% black rabbit dubbing, 10% black Flashabou dubbing.

Hackle: Black genetic hen, wound palmer style.
Rib: Fine copper wire, wound in opposite direction to hackle.
Head: Small to medium gold bead.
Tying tip: Brush out fur dubbing to give the fly a buggy, scruffy look.
Commercially tied alternatives: None; this is one you will have to tie yourself, although it is a quick and easy pattern, and if it ends up looking a bit untidy – well, the trout will like it all the better!
When and how to fish this pattern: The Soft Hackle Woolly worm is a very heavily weighted fly designed to plummet through strong currents. The high visibility of this pattern ensures trout can see it in discoloured water. Effective both as a down-and-across streamer pattern using a lively retrieve, and for upstream dead-drifting with a strike indicator.

HEAVY HALF BACK
Originator: Frank Schlosser, NZ. **Variant:** Fred Steynberg, SA.
Hook: 14, 12 Tiemco 3761 or similar 2× long, heavy-wire nymph hook.
Thread: 6/0 dark brown.
Weight: 5 to 15 turns lead wire.
Tail: Mix of brown and dark dun hackle fibres.
Abdomen: Partly stripped peacock herl.
Rib: Fine copper wire.

Thorax: Peacock herl.
Hackle: Dark brown cock hackle.
Wing case: Pearl Mylar.
Tying tip: To make the fly more durable, wind a few turns of thread through the peacock herl and hackle in the thorax before you tie down the wing case at the eye of the hook.
Commercially tied alternatives: I have not seen this pattern on sale. Tom Sutcliffe's widely available and very effective Zak nymph is an excellent alternative.
When and how to fish this pattern: Although similar to the Zak Nymph, I believe the Heavy Half Back offers an advantage in slow or very clear water when a more realistic pattern is required. Fish upstream dead-drift with a strike indicator. In very clear water, I often team a size 14 Heavy Half Back with a size 18 unweighted Spring Creek Pheasant Tail Nymph as the point fly.

PEACOCK WOOLLY WORM
Originator: Traditional pattern originally from the USA, the peacock version was popularised in South Africa by Hugh Huntley.
Hook: 12, 10, Tiemco 3761 or similar 2× long, heavy-wire nymph hook.
Weight: 4 to 10 turns lead wire.
Thread: 6/0 black.
Tail: Black hen, wound palmer style.
Body: 3 or 4 strands bronze peacock herl.
Hackle: Black hen, wound palmer style.

Rib: Fine copper wire, wound in opposite direction to hackle.
Head: Black glass bead or gold metal bead.
Tying tip: Dead easy and quick to tie. I use a black bead for the lighter versions, and a gold bead for the heavy ones, so that I can easily tell them apart.
Commercially available alternatives: You may not easily get the peacock version in the shops, but any black dubbed Woolly Worm will work almost as well. Like the Woolly Bugger, innumerable versions of this fly have been tied over the years. The problem with shop flies for river nymphing is that some are weighted – but most are not, so you will have to take what you can get.
When and how to fish this pattern: Most effective fished upstream dead-drift with a strike indicator. Best in rivers with good populations of dragonfly nymphs. I often fish the weighted Peacock Woolly Worm teamed with a small Hare's Ear or Pheasant Tail Nymph as the point fly.

HUMPY
Originator: Jack Horner, USA.
Hook: 16, 14, 12, standard dry fly.
Thread: Yellow 6/0.
Tail, shellback and wings: Brown deer hair.
Body: Yellow tying silk is the standard dressing. Try a fluorescent orange wool body for dirty water.
Hackle: Grizzly and brown genetic cock hackles.
Tying tips: I think everyone will agree that

the Humpy is a pig to tie! The shellback and wings are formed from one length of deer hair, so the proportions are critical when you first tie in the shellback. I find it best to spend an evening tying only Humpies (this usually gives me enough to last about two years) and after some trial and error the proportions come out right. A little Dave's Flexament applied to the shellback makes the fly more durable.
Commercially tied alternatives: This pattern is widely commercially available.
When and how to fish this pattern: My first choice as a dry searching pattern – especially when there is no visible surface activity. Who knows exactly what it imitates – maybe a big beetle or grasshopper badly beaten up in the current? The Humpy will often draw non-rising fish holding deep, and can be regarded as an attractor dry fly rather than an imitative pattern.

ELK HAIR CADDIS
Originator: Al Troth, USA.
Hook: 18, 16, 14, 12, standard dry fly.
Thread: Brown 6/0 or 8/0.
Tail: None.
Body: Pale grey hare underfur.
Hackle: Grizzly genetic cock hackle wound palmer style. Recent versions of this fly often omit the palmered hackle altogether.
Rib: Very fine gold wire.
Underwing: Natural CDC (optional).

Overwing: Elk or deer hair.
Tying tips: Try not to flare the hair wing too much. When tying in the wing, use gentle tension on the thread for the last few turns. Caddis adults can vary from pale grey or tan, right through to very dark brown. I keep things simple by tying only two versions of the Elk Hair Caddis – a light one and a dark version. This fly is also deadly on dams during a caddis hatch. On still waters, I prefer a low-floating version, created by clipping away the hackle flush with the body (or omit the hackle altogether).
When and how to fish this pattern: If you see *any* caddis activity – a hatch or just a few adults in the riverside vegetation – then the Elk Hair Caddis is the pattern to use. Also a good searching fly, even when no caddis are present. Fish upstream dry with a dead-drift. During a heavy caddis hatch, a downstream cast with a skittered retrieve may draw a lot of strikes.

HUNTING TROPHY TROUT

A big trout making a big splash. I can understand Roger's look of concern at landing this fish – although fortunately it was soon in the net. Fertile dams managed for trophy trout are often intentionally lightly stocked, so you may have to fish long and hard for such an opportunity.

WHAT IS A TRUE TROPHY TROUT?

In this short chapter, I'm going to focus on the fish that have 'grown on' in dams, in other words, trout that have been stocked as fry or fingerlings and become huge by rich, natural feeding. I'm going to exclude hatchery fish fed to an enormous size on pellets and introduced into dams as 'instant trophies'. I'm also excluding dams where growth is enhanced by pellet feeding – resulting in much larger fish than the water could ever naturally produce. This is purely an aesthetic preference on my part. I have caught more 10-pound-plus fish from pellet-enhanced fisheries than 'grown-on' waters. The pellet-fed trout were exciting to catch, and difficult too, as they had undoubtedly been caught and released many times previously. Somehow, though, I don't feel I can 'count' these fish (not that I really like to keep tallies anyway, but I think you know what I mean). However, I believe that the individual should decide where to draw the line. I don't want to prescribe on the ethics of this matter; *you* decide, and if you want to include huge pellet-fed trout in *your* tally then by all means, do so.

I class any stillwater trout over 5 pounds as a 'nice one'. Six- and 7-pound trout are 'big' by my reckoning. I have caught lots of (grown-on) trout of this size over the years, and most fertile, well-managed fisheries are capable of producing 7-ounders. The cut-off point seems to come at around 8 pounds. I have caught far fewer 8 pounders, and when we come to 9-pounders, I think I could probably count them on the fingers of one hand.

For 10-pound-plus grown-on fish, my total is exactly two in more than three decades of fly-fishing. So, I believe any trout of 8 pounds plus can be considered a trophy – and this would apply pretty much anywhere in the world.

TROPHY TROUT WATERS

Finding waters that hold true trophies is not easy. Of course many anglers (and fishery owners too!) claim, 'Oh, yes, there

At over 100 hectares, Lifton Lake at Sani Valley Lodge near Underberg is a huge expanse of water with a reputation for equally big trout. Over the years, many 10-pounders have come from this dam. As with all large waters, you may need to spend time searching for the hot spots.

are *huge* trout in this dam, they have just become too clever to catch.' This is possible of course, but I believe it unlikely. When experienced anglers regularly fish a dam, the big ones *do* eventually get caught. Since I began writing this book, I have had a sonar fish finder fitted to my kick boat. The sonar gives a fairly accurate indication of fish size. Extensive use of the sonar confirms what I have long suspected. *Many* dams hold 5- and 6-pound trout, but *very few* grow on fish to the 8-pound-plus trophy size. This explains why we catch 5- and 6-pounders pretty regularly from my local KwaZulu-Natal waters, but few huge trophies – simply because they are rarely present.

For a dam to grow truly huge fish, many factors need to come together at the same time. The dam must, of course, be highly fertile, with extensive weedy shallows, as well as some deep water in which the fish can find refuge during hot spells. It would need to be lightly stocked, so that there is little competition for food. Also – and this is very important – fishing pressure will need to be light, and/or catch and release strictly enforced. Otherwise all the trout will get

whopped on the head and taken out long before they have a chance to become trophy-sized.

The timing of weather cycles is also an important factor in catching trophies. A series of wet, cool summers followed by mild winters will greatly accelerate growth rates. For example, Mpumalanga and KwaZulu-Natal experienced a very hot dry summer in 2003/4. I believe some of the Mpumalanga waters were badly affected by the heat. My local waters still produced plenty of medium-sized trout, but even 6-pounders were few and far between compared with our catches in the mid- to late 1990s. Then the summers were wetter and cooler.

Much like property investment, the key to success is location, location, location -- both in terms of fishing the right waters and finding the trout in trophy dams. Currently, the hot areas for big fish include some of the East Griqualand dams and the relatively new Eastern Cape trout still waters in the Stormberg and Winterberg regions. A couple of years ago, we were hearing about huge fish from the Kouebokkeveld dams north of Ceres in the Western Cape, as well as Sani Valley

Lodge and a few other dams near Underberg in KwaZulu-Natal. Waters tend to go in cycles, so if you want to catch a monster it is a good idea to watch reports in the local angling magazines and get onto the 'grapevine' of other serious big-trout hunters. You may need to do lots of travelling to fish waters that are currently in a peak big-fish cycle.

TROPHY TACTICS

As far as trophy trout tactics are concerned, finding the fish is a prime factor – even more so than it is when fishing for average-sized trout. The chances are that the trout will have become huge because there are not all that many of them. In the Mastering Stillwaters chapter, page 28, I mentioned that 70% of the trout are likely to be located in 30% of a dam. On a lightly stocked trophy dam, this ratio could easily shift to 80% of the fish holding in just 20% of the dam.

On many trophy dams, the fish seldom rise to a mayfly or midge hatch; they don't need to – there will be tons of larger, more nutritious food items below the surface. You will need to draw on all your accumulated knowledge to locate unseen fish by understanding structure, temperature and oxygen needs, and food concentrations. Sonar is a big help – not so much in actually seeing trout on the screen (you will be right above them in your kick boat when they appear on the sonar monitor, so they are likely to be spooked); rather, sonar can give a very valuable insight into finding fish-holding structure, such as the channels, drop-offs and weedbeds, where you should concentrate your efforts.

TROPHY FLIES AND GEAR

Lastly, fly patterns and gear. Don't mess around with light stuff. I have never felt the need for a rod more powerful than a 5 weight, but when you are fishing for trophies, strong tippets are essential. The lightest I use for big fish is 2× fluorocarbon. If there is heavy weed growth, and there probably will be, then 1× or even 0× will give you a better chance of bullying a 10-pounder out of trouble.

Fish get big in rich waters by feeding on abundant large food items. Large dragon nymph imitations, Woolly Buggers and, if minnows are present, fry-imitating patterns are the best bet. My biggest ever 'grown-on' rainbow at 11 pounds 4 ounces fell to a size 8 Olive Filoplume Dragon. Second best at 10 pounds 12 ounces came to a Black Variegated Chenille Woolly Bugger, also a size 8. Neither flies are by any means exotic patterns. As I said before, the key to catching a trophy is location, location, location – plus, of course, stopping that monster from diving into a weedbed when you do finally hook it!

The lower reaches of our trout rivers can also offer the chance of a larger-than-average fish. Fish densities are likely to be low, so it would pay to cover a lot of water quickly, using streamer patterns.

CATCH AND RELEASE

Always unhook a fish in the water (left). It is a good idea to have a pair of artery forceps handy to gain a better grip on the hook. If you wish to weigh a fish (right), do so in the net, but make sure that you get it back into the water very quickly.

In the States, catch and release is practised with an almost religious fervor, and is regarded as the *only way* to preserve wild trout stocks under heavy fishing pressure. In this country, the concept of releasing most, if not all of the trout caught, still draws some controversy. Opponents to the catch-and-release ethic are of the opinion that many fish will die after a day or two anyway. Others claim that they want to 'get their money's worth' out of fishing, by taking trout home to eat. The latter argument, in particular, makes no sense to me. If you want to eat trout it will *always* be cheaper to go to the supermarket and buy them. Taking into account the cost of tackle and flies, etc., plus petrol and fishing fees, you would never come close breaking even. I get *my* money's worth just from the sheer joy of being out on the water. Also, trout look a lot prettier to me swimming off strongly after a successful release, than they do lying dead on the bank.

Regarding fish mortality, there have been instances of numbers of fish dying following a group of anglers having had a 'busy day' on the water. I am convinced that this was a result of bad technique, or fishing when waters temperatures were too high. Studies in the States indicate a catch-and-release mortality rate of 4% on public waters (where you could expect a great variation in levels of skill among anglers). Experienced anglers releasing fish with great care would, I believe, reduce this figure significantly.

A tagging program at a private Underberg dam has shown repeated capture of trophy-sized trout over a period of months – with one fish even being caught twice in one day! It is very likely that we often catch a trout that has been caught and released before, but do not realise it because the fish has no distinguishing marks. My own experience of certain repeated capture includes a 6-pound 8-ounce rainbow that I caught three times last winter, and a 5-pounder I released five times over a period of nine months a couple of years ago. Both fish had scars from a close shave with a cormorant or heron when they were smaller, and so were easy to identify. So catch and release does work. Indeed, I firmly believe it is the only way to preserve wild trout stocks or to have large 'grown-on' fish in waters that see moderate to heavy fishing pressure.

Here are a few pointers that will help you to ensure successful catch and release:

- **PLAY FISH HARD AND FAST.** This is the *key factor* in successful release. Long fights result in a lactic acid build-up in the trout's body, greatly reducing its chance of survival (*see* Fighting fish in the Mastering Stillwaters chapter, page 45).

- **HEAVY TIPPETS** are essential to put serious pressure on a fish. The excellent abrasion and shock resistance of fluorocarbon offers a distinct advantage over conventional nylon monofilament.

- **FISH BARBLESS HOOKS,** or pinch down the barb with pliers to minimise damage. If you are concerned about fish 'falling off' when fishing barbless, then compromise by just turning down the barb slightly, but still leave a 'bump' where the barb was. I find this works very well, as fish are less likely to come off during the fight, and yet the hooks are easy to remove. Always have a pair of artery forceps handy to assist in hook removal. I *never* tie trout flies on hooks larger than a size 8. Large hooks penetrate too deeply and may cause great damage.

- **USE A SOFT MESH NET.** If you still have one of the old hard-knotted nylon nets, please replace it. Knotted nylon nets will split fins, and scrape off scales and the fish's protective slime. An alternative is not to net the fish at all, and to rather use a quick-release tool such as the Ketchum Release (you slide the tool down the line and push out the hook without having to handle the fish at all). I find these work okay for small fish of up to 2 pounds. A big fish needs to be played right out to be able to use a release tool. I prefer to bully a big trout into a net quickly, where it is easier to control and remove the hook.

Trout may need a little recovery time. Hold the fish firmly by the tail until it makes a determined effort to swim away.

- **DON'T TAKE THEM OUT OF THE WATER AT ALL IF YOU CAN HELP IT.** After netting a fish, remove the hook *while the net is still in the water.* If you want to weigh a trout, do so very quickly by weighing it in the net (but don't forget to deduct the weight of the net!). Try not to hoist the fish out of the water for more than two or three seconds. Likewise, if you want a photograph, get the camera ready and set up before you take the fish out of the water. Better still, photograph the trout *in* the water – as I have done for many images in this book. It is thought that a trout removed from the water for 30 seconds has only a 50% chance of survival. If you are not going to weigh or photograph a fish there is really no reason to take it out of the water at all.

- **DON'T SQUEEZE.** A trout has delicate organs along its body that are easily damaged if you grip tightly. The *only* place you can safely hold a fish firmly is by the 'wrist' of the tail.

- **REVIVAL.** A tired trout sometimes needs a little time to recover after being landed. If you release an exhausted fish it will most likely sink down into the weeds and 'give up'. Hold the fish firmly by the wrist of the tail and gently support it beneath the belly with your other hand if necessary (hold the trout facing upstream if you are fishing a river). Wait until the trout is making determined attempts to swim and then let it go. In some cases, it might take several minutes for the fish to recover its strength. It may help to push the fish forward to increase the flow of water through the gills, and then slowly pull it back, repeating this procedure until it shows signs of being ready to swim off. Small fish of under a pound should need very little, if any, recovery time. Even trout of 3 or 4 pounds should be ready for release in a few moments if they have been landed quickly. It is also essential to release fish into *clear, open water.* If you are bank fishing, this means wading beyond the margin weeds; a fish released into weed may also give up. The aim is to get a released fish to swim away strongly – and to keep on swimming. Its chances of survival will then be excellent.

- **WATER TEMPERATURE** is also a big factor for successful release. At temperatures below 18°C, most fish recover easily. Between 18 and 21°C catch and release is possible but the fish must be played very quickly, and should be carefully revived. At 22°C and above, oxygen levels are low, and trout become heat stressed – resulting in a very high mortality rate for released fish. I don't trout fish in dams when the water is above 21°C. Instead, I choose a high-altitude river where the water is likely to be cooler and better oxygenated. Alternatively, I switch to fly-fishing for warm-water species such as bass or yellowfish.

THE IMPATIENT FLYFISHER

Don't flog away at one spot – whether you are fishing a dam or a river. Move, and keep moving, until you find the prime trout-holding areas. In the case of rivers and streams, it is common practice to cover several kilometres of water in a day.

The common wisdom about folk who fish is that we have infinite patience. 'Oh, so you go fishing – well you must have *lots* of patience!' In many aspects of life I have very little patience indeed – traffic jams, long queues at the bank, and computer crashes would be good examples.

When I am in the natural world, I do take things much steadier – simply because I love being there.

However, fly-fishing differs from many other forms of angling in that it is especially proactive. There are an enormous number of variables that you can experiment with in order to achieve success. Therefore, when fly-fishing, I believe it is possible to be *too* patient. In a dam or stream that holds a good head of trout, you should expect to get some action – and fairly quickly, if conditions are favourable.

If nothing is happening, think about making a *change* in the way you are fishing. The first thing I would change is where I am fishing. So, if I am not getting takes or seeing signs of feeding fish, I move to a fresh area, and keep on moving until I find some activity.

I often see anglers flog away at one spot for hours just because they have caught trout there in the past. Remember: food, security and temperature all have a profound effect on where trout are to be found. And these factors are all subject to constant change, so the trout will go where present conditions suit them.

My next move would be to alter presentation, such as varying fishing depth and retrieve. Even just a small tweak in retrieve style or depth of presentation can suddenly make things come alive. Switching fly patterns can also make a big

Presentation is a key factor when fishing. If you aren't getting action, try varying the depth and speed of retrieve. Even just a small tweak in these variables can suddenly make things come alive. Keep experimenting until you find the right formula for the current conditions.

Sometimes the difficult, slow days can be the most rewarding – when you eventually figure out the winning tactics.

difference, of course, but on waters that I know well, this is my last resort. I give the flies that have been consistently successful in the past a good try before I start changing patterns.

Making a decision as to exactly which tactics to employ on a particular day is the tough part. You can reason it out to a certain extent, by taking into account current conditions, but trout can be contrary creatures. Just to keep us on our toes, they often do the opposite of what we might logically expect. This is where intuition – gut feel, if you like – plays a huge role in consistent success. Fly-fishers who have the uncanny ability to catch trout just about anywhere at anytime – even when everyone else is getting absolutely zip – all seem to have a finely tuned intuitive sense. The best way to enhance intuition is to fish a lot, and to gain experience on as many different waters as possible. This builds a reservoir of knowledge over the years.

I have just given you an excellent excuse to fish more often – so get out there and enjoy it.

Happy fly-fishing!

BUGS AND KNOTS

A QUICK GUIDE TO AQUATIC INSECTS

I subscribe to the school of thought that says trout don't know the Latin names of the bugs they eat, so fly-fishers don't really need to learn them either. However, a basic knowledge of trout foods can help in understanding trout behaviour, plus, of course, give a few pointers as to which flies to use.

It can be very useful to be able to look at a bug and say, okay, this is a mayfly dun, caddis pupa, dragonfly nymph, etc. The table below focuses on widespread aquatic insects commonly eaten by trout. Terrestrial insects also find their way onto the water and into a trout's stomach. I have not illustrated these – I am sure we all know what grasshoppers, beetles and ants look like. Likewise, other familiar aquatic items commonly on the trout's menu such as minnows, frogs and snails. The aquatic subadult stages of insects would typically be imitated with nymph patterns, and are high-lighted in the green boxes. The adult winged forms appear in the blue boxes; you would, of course, use a dry fly for these.

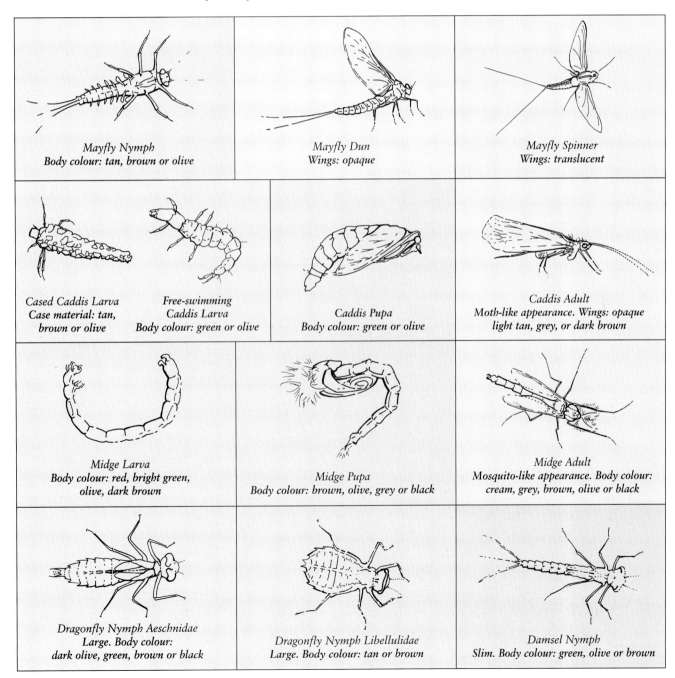

Mayfly Nymph
Body colour: tan, brown or olive

Mayfly Dun
Wings: opaque

Mayfly Spinner
Wings: translucent

Cased Caddis Larva
Case material: tan, brown or olive

Free-swimming Caddis Larva
Body colour: green or olive

Caddis Pupa
Body colour: green or olive

Caddis Adult
Moth-like appearance. Wings: opaque light tan, grey, or dark brown

Midge Larva
Body colour: red, bright green, olive, dark brown

Midge Pupa
Body colour: brown, olive, grey or black

Midge Adult
Mosquito-like appearance. Body colour: cream, grey, brown, olive or black

Dragonfly Nymph Aeschnidae
Large. Body colour: dark olive, green, brown or black

Dragonfly Nymph Libellulidae
Large. Body colour: tan or brown

Damsel Nymph
Slim. Body colour: green, olive or brown

ESSENTIAL KNOTS

The knots shown below are the ones that I use for both nylon monofilament and fluorocarbon.

You need to be especially careful with fluorocarbon and other high-strength materials, as many of the old knots – such as the barrel knot used to join two pieces of tippet – are unreliable.

With all knots it is important to moisten with saliva or, better still, lubricate with lip balm before *slowly* tightening the knot.

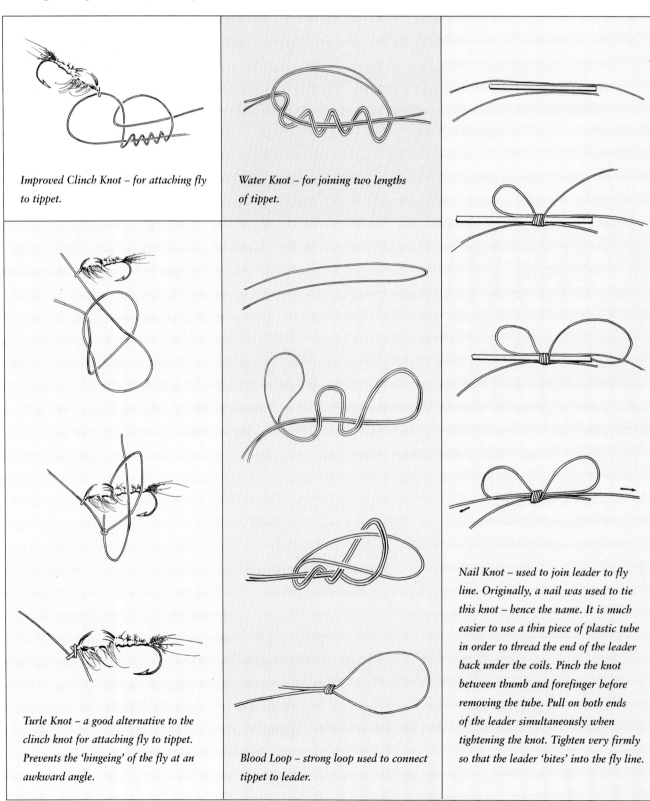

Improved Clinch Knot – for attaching fly to tippet.

Water Knot – for joining two lengths of tippet.

Turle Knot – a good alternative to the clinch knot for attaching fly to tippet. Prevents the 'hingeing' of the fly at an awkward angle.

Blood Loop – strong loop used to connect tippet to leader.

Nail Knot – used to join leader to fly line. Originally, a nail was used to tie this knot – hence the name. It is much easier to use a thin piece of plastic tube in order to thread the end of the leader back under the coils. Pinch the knot between thumb and forefinger before removing the tube. Pull on both ends of the leader simultaneously when tightening the knot. Tighten very firmly so that the leader 'bites' into the fly line.

BIBLIOGRAPHY

ARNOLD, PAUL. 1998. *Wisdom of the Guides.* Frank Amato, USA.

BEST, AK. 1996. *A.K.'s Fly Box.* Lyons Press, USA.

BORGER, JASON. 2001. *Nature of Fly Casting.* Shadow Caster Press, USA.

CAIRNCROSS, MARTIN AND DAWSON, JOHN. 2000. *Trout Fly Fishing – An Expert Approach.* Swan Hill Press, UK.

CHURCH, BOB. 1995. *Guide to New Fly Patterns.* Crowood Press, UK.

CHURCH, BOB AND GATERCOLE, PETER. 1995. *Fly Fishing for Trout.* Crowood Press, UK.

CLARKE, BRIAN AND GODDARD, JOHN. 1980. *The Trout and the Fly.* Page Bros, UK.

GIERACH, JOHN. 1989. *Fly Fishing Small Streams.* Stackpole Books, USA.

GIERACH, JOHN. 2000. *Good Flies.* Lyons Press, USA.

GODDARD, JOHN. 2002. *Reflections of a Game Fisher.* Robert Hale, UK.

HUGHS, DAVE. 1995. *Nymph Fishing.* Frank Amato, USA.

HUGHS, DAVE. 1988. *Reading the Water.* Stackpole Books, USA.

HUGHS, DAVE. 2000. *Essential Trout Flies.* Stackpole Books, USA.

HUGHS, DAVE. 2002. *Trout from Small Streams.* Stackpole Books, USA.

JARDINE, CHARLES. 1991. *The Sotherby's Guide to Fly-fishing for Trout.* Dorling Kindersley, UK.

KITE, OLIVER. 1963. *Nymph Fishing in Practice.* Barrie & Jenkins, UK.

LEE, ART. 1999. *Lore of Trout Fishing.* Human Kinetics, USA.

LEESON, TOM. 1994. *The Habit of Rivers.* Lyons & Burford, USA.

McGUANE, THOMAS. 1999. *The Longest Silence.* Vintage Books, USA.

MORRIS, SKIP AND CHAN, BRIAN. 1999. *Fly Fishing Trout Lakes.* Frank Amato, USA.

OSTOFF, RICH. 2001. *No Hatch to Match.* Stackpole Books, USA.

PATTERSON, NEIL. 1995. *Chalkstream Chronicle.* Merlin Unwin Books, UK.

RICKARDS, DENNY. 1997. *Fly-fishing Stillwaters for Trophy Trout.* Stillwater Productions, USA .

RIPHAGEN, DEAN. 1998. *The South African Fly Fishing Handbook.* New Holland, RSA.

ROSENBAUER, TOM. 2000. *The Orvis Guide to Prospecting for Trout.* Lyons Press, USA.

SCHOLLMEYER, JIM. 2001. *Nymph fly-tying Techniques.* Frank Amato, USA.

SHEWEY, JOHN. 1994. *Mastering the Spring Creeks.* Frank Amato, USA.

STEEVES, HARRISION R AND KOCH, ED. 1994. *Terrestrials.* Stackpole Books, USA.

SUTCLIFFE, TOM. 1990. *Reflections on Flyfishing.* Mark and Ronald Basil, RSA.

SUTCLIFFE, TOM. 2002. *Hunting Trout.* Freestone Press, RSA.

SWISHER, DOUG AND RICHARDS, CARL. 1971. *Selective Trout.* Lyons Press, USA.

TRAVER, ROBERT. 1974. *Trout Magic.* Simon & Schuster, USA.

TULLIS, LARRY. 2003. *Small Fly Techniques.* Lyons Press, USA.

WRIGHT, LEONARD M. 1996. *Trout Maverick.* Lyons & Burford, USA.

INDEX